Barbara Briggs Morrow

Publications International, Ltd.

Barbara Briggs Morrow is a contributing editor and senior writer for *Midwest Living* magazine and a veteran travel writer and editor whose work has appeared in *Cosmopolitan, Christian Science Monitor,* and *The Des Moines Register*. In the course of researching articles for newspapers, magazines, and books, she has explored country roads in every region. She was a contributing writer for the book *20 Great Weekend Getaways*.

Editorial Assistance: Robert T. Briggs

→ Contents ←

America's Heart Journeys Home   4

Not too far from bustling steel-and-glass cities, there stretches a vast wilderness that tantalizes us, just as it did the pioneers. As you journey, the countryside startles you with its dramatic shifts in character from region to region, and the land glimmers with the spirit that built this nation—and enables it to endure.

The Northeast   8

From the moment the Pilgrims first set foot on the craggy Massachusetts shore, facing the teeth of a howling New England winter, it was a foretelling of the struggles to come. The Northeast's independent, inventive spirit sparked the nation's first industries. But almost in the shadow of cities that pride themselves in balancing on the cutting edge, the rural Northeast seems to be a place left behind and glad of it.

The South   64

Old-fashioned Southern hospitality goes beyond mere politeness to genuine caring. As long as you're not in a hurry, an old-time welcome awaits in these places where the Old South's heritage comes alive. In these parts, folks cherish their families and their pasts—and their reverence to the land runs deep.

The Midwest   108

Every inch of plowed grassland, every plot cleared of timber, and every rough-hewn cabin or tiny settlement in the Midwest represents a hard-fought battle. You'll find the heartland spirit not only in barns, in farmhouse kitchens, and in white-frame country churches, but also in the unspoiled places where deer and wildflowers flourish.

The West   164

The West endures as the United States' last frontier. Huge chunks of this territory remain not just untamed, but untouched. The giant landscape, from sprawling plains to mile-high peaks to lush vineyards, calls us westward, just as it did the adventurous settlers who first made that arduous trip more than a century ago.

AMERICA'S HEART
JOURNEYS HOME

City life can take on a gray-tinged sameness. Look-alike cars speed along slabs of concrete so similar that without the billboards and green highway signs you might not be able to guess whether you're in Los Angeles or Chicago. Downtown (it hardly matters which one), towers of glass and steel rise anonymously, uniform in their studied angles and gleaming surfaces. Pedestrians charge along sidewalks in solitary crowds. The veteran rushers look neither right nor left, knowing there's nothing to see that they haven't seen before and probably couldn't see down the block.

Evenings, everyone rushes in the opposite direction, eager to retreat to the suburbs. Colors, furnishings, pictures hanging on the walls make these places our own. But the settings—brick rectangles or replicated Cape Cods, surrounded by similar-sized plots—vary little from one metropolitan area to another. Various appliances separate you from daily drudgery, and communication devices fill your every free moment.

TV newscasters breeze over the weather forecast. Traffic reports fill much of the time that once went to the weather. Most of the time, it doesn't matter much. Air-conditioning or heating keeps the tempera-

Above: *Tree boughs not quite leafed out in early summer shelter this old covered bridge, too tiny to allow much time for the kissing that is supposed to be one of a covered bridge's chief attractions. In a month or so, the foliage will hide this old-timer almost completely.* Opposite page: *A sugary snowfall blankets the banks of Glade Creek near the working grist mill in West Virginia's Babcock State Park.*

ture hovering around an ideal 70 degrees. There's no reason to spend extended periods outside, so rain and snow become pesky—but hardly noticeable—inconveniences. Seasons shift, and unless you make it a point

Franciscan friars lovingly built the Mission of the Pueblo de Laguna to minister to the Indians in New Mexico. Almost three centuries later, the simple church endures, serving a congregation of more than 7,000 on a reservation east of Albuquerque. The pastor celebrates mass for his enormous flock twice a day.

to break out of your routine, you don't have to acknowledge the difference.

You almost could begin to think from this frantic, insular existence that life as most of our great grandparents knew it has disappeared. When we have a few moments to think—maybe caught in traffic or staring at the first balmy spring day through double-paned plate glass—we can't help longing for that world we fear is lost. This publication grew out of that longing.

This is about a gentler world that endures surprisingly close to the city's bustle. It is just a few miles, in some cases, from the freeway or a little beyond the manicured suburbs. To find it, you might follow a road that's twisting and no longer smooth. You might strike

off from the paved path altogether, into silent woods across a field bobbing with black-eyed Susans.

What you discover depends on where you are. Beyond the cities, a vast land stretches. Here, you still can find some of the wildness that tantalized the pioneers, and the countryside captivates you with its shifts in character and regional idiosyncrasies. Waves crash against craggy New England shores little changed since the Pilgrims landed more than three centuries ago. In the South, spreading oaks trail gray beards of moss, bathing white-columned plantation houses in puddles of shade. A neat patchwork of farm fields covers much of the country's center. Further west, wide-open spaces—sun-bleached and level—stretch to the horizon and peaks unchanged in millennia touch the sky.

Generations of people have made their mark on these lands, but their imprints mostly harmonize with the land's character: Cornfields stretch for miles as the prairies once did, and villages nestle at an old fording place on a stream or in a valley's welcoming crook. Here, you'll see a state somewhere between shiny new and shabby. Barns built to last generations ago weather to a silver sheen, a hue that carries its own charm like the color of a beloved grandmother's hair. Churches and farmhouses long settled so corners rest slightly askew proudly wear the latest in uncounted coats of sparkling white. Covered bridges that sheltered courting couples a century ago creak under the weight of motorized steel but companionably shoulder the load like old friends asked for an unexpected favor.

On these back roads, when you pass another car, or more likely a pickup, the driver probably will raise a hand. No, it's no one you know. But in these parts, you might not share a road often, and it's an occasion worth noting. On village streets, you can try hurrying along, eyes glazed like a curtain drawn against the outside, the way most of us have learned to do on city streets. Folks probably will say hello anyway. If you appear to be in too much of a rush, someone might ask you if anything's wrong and if you need some help.

If you stop to buy something, the shopkeeper or clerk will chat about the heat or the cold or the storm that's moving this way. Here, the weather matters. Folks study the sky with concentration reserved for the morning sports page in the city and feel shifts in the breeze as surely as subway riders notice when someone brushes against them. There's nothing idle about this interest. Rain mires the fields and costs the farmer a day's work. A gale churns the sea and chases the fisher back to the harbor. Snow piles up on country roads, stopping the world as surely as if it had been packed in cotton batting, keeping children home from school and sending homemakers to their pantries to check their stores.

The seasons transform this landscape, so that you might not recognize the same spot in May and in October. Winter casts northern lands in sparkling, shimmering alabaster. Spring blooms soft as snowy dogwood blossoms but as insistent as the new green of sprouting grass. Summer, lush and fragrant, lulls the land into a lazy drowse. Fall sets fire to unassuming woodlands, turning shady, looping back roads into corridors of flaming crimson and flashing gold.

Turning these pages, you'll explore the country's back roads and visit America's venerable places from New England's harbors and old-time covered bridges to the South's majestic houses and barns that still bear advertising slogans as if television hadn't ever been invented. You'll see churches faithfully serving their congregations after two centuries and lighthouses standing guard over treacherous shores. But most important, on each of these places—in the carefully restored one-room schoolhouse, in the barn that refuses to fall down even after years of neglect, in the painstakingly plowed farm furrows, and in lands still wild and untamed—you'll see glimmers of the spirit that built this nation and help it to endure. It is a world you might have feared is lost, a world you can visit again and again.

The brilliant, ruddy canopy near this barn in New Jersey suggests that it is almost time to reap another hard-earned harvest in the Garden State.

THE NORTHEAST

Scratch the surface of the Northeastern United States and you'll scrape rough bedrock. Plows push through the region's meager covering of glacier-deposited soil, only to bang against the earth's granite backbone. Newcomers press natives beyond vague pleasantries and squarely strike stone-solid independence and iron surety of what's right—qualities upon which this country was built.

The Northeast's independent, inventive spirit sparked the nation's first industries—mills powered by streams rushing through the rugged countryside. Many ports and factory towns burgeoned into cities that have become world centers of trade and commerce. But if you look past these racing, glittering centers, you will find a Northeast that the plain-living, hard-working founders would recognize.

Almost in the shadow of cities that pride themselves on balancing on the cutting edge, the rural Northeast seems to be a place left behind and glad of it. Woodlands and glassy lakes still claim millions of acres. Country roads skirt walls built of stones that preceding generations of farmers carried one by one from the fields. On New England farmsteads, carefully crafted barns and simple, frame houses huddle together as they have for generations. To the west, prosperous dairy operations sprawl across the rolling landscape of New York state and Pennsylvania, featuring cavernous barns reigning like castles over the rich land.

On the shore, fishers still take their living from the sea, and waves lap against solitary beaches where the only sounds you'll hear are rushing water and calling

Opposite page: *Deacon Jonathan Elkins founded the town of Peacham, Vermont, in 1775 and named the village after Peckham, England. Peacham prospered, and grateful citizens built the church that still presides over the village green.*
Above: *The graves of this 19th-century family rest in a carefully tended plot on Pemaquid Point, Maine.*

gulls. Forested hills frame white clapboard towns nestled around tree-shaded village greens. Town meetings—free-wheeling gatherings where everyone has his or her say—decide community questions. On Sundays, the bell tolling in the steeple of the church on the commons calls the congregation to services just as it has since the country's earliest days.

The Pilgrims first set foot on this region's coast, stepping gingerly onto the craggy Massachusetts shore into the teeth of a howling, New England winter. It was a beginning that foretold struggles to come. On the coast, these immigrants bravely confronted the cruel whims of the sea, stretching sparkling and smooth one day and churning into a fury the next, pounding newborn ports and splintering the stoutest ships like toys. Inland, farmers cleared towering hardwoods and unyielding thicket. Fighting to etch furrows into hilly fields, settlers parted rocky earth only to find more rocks underneath.

Only the flintiest managed to chisel success out of this inhospitable land; others moved on at the first chance, setting out for more tranquil shores to the south or more welcoming soil to the west. In those who stayed, the effort forged determination and self-reliance—long before the crown decided to take its recalci-

trant Colonies in hand. Imagine the shock of King George's polished regiments! Expecting to face a rag-tag collection of Colonial farmers and merchants, the British regulars slammed into granite resistance, a fierce fighting spirit that no amount of training could produce.

These staunchly self-reliant pioneers prized religion and learning. Even though they themselves still were living in rough cabins, founders of new towns built churches and schools. These buildings held places of honor on the village green, a common space set aside for public gatherings. Everyone took as a matter of course that many such gatherings would be necessary. No community issue could be decided without hearing all points of view. These immigrants had paid a dear price for this freedom, and only a fool would consider not exercising his precious rights.

Even after wealth and hard-earned leisure might have allowed for some curlicues and gingerbread, the Northeast's builders chose classic designs and painted their public buildings and homes white—plain and unadorned. Simple spires rose gracefully over clapboard

September sets fire to towering maples along this winding two-lane country byway near Stockbridge, Massachusetts.

churches. Homes, dependably square with windows lined up in balanced rows, presented facades welcoming in their lack of artifice. These structures were built to last, and the builders' descendants placed a high value on such legacies of the past. Ever practical and prudent, they also were wary of change for its own sake and frivolous new styles.

Wearing fresh coats of gleaming white, 19th-century structures—from churches to homes to country inns—still dot the Northeast. Old-fashioned covered bridges cross the rivers and streams. Some are gussied up with new boards and fresh paint. Others unabashedly show their age, wood gray and worn and broken boards letting in sun or rain. Mills that early entrepreneurs built to harness water power preside over tumbling streams. Some of these old-timers have been restored so you can see how the grinding stones work, take home a pound of freshly ground flour, or just enjoy watching the water splash over the creaking wheel.

In the last century, vacationers discovered the shore towns. Victorian cottages now house bed-and-breakfasts. Shops selling artists' and crafters' works share main streets with purveyors of practical goods. Year-round residents welcome the summer people and the winter ski buffs with a sort of tight-lipped tolerance that wonders what all this vacationing is about. But it's a welcome nonetheless. Truth be told, some of these crusty year-rounders started out as visitors themselves.

Locals and visitors alike savor each season's passing. Following the lush green of spring and the hard, hot summer, fall sets fire to much of the Northeast, crimsons and golds blazing across forested

The Pemaquid Point Lighthouse has stood its lonely vigil on the Maine coast since 1827—a watch made more solitary since the Coast Guard automated the faithful beam in 1934.

hills and maples exploding with color like Roman candles amid peaceful villages. Winter blankets the region in glistening white, imposing a stillness that Northeasterners prize.

Historic sites preserve the country's beginnings as if in trust for the rest of the nation. Faithful guardians—ordinary folks, often unpaid and unsung—tend to these landmarks. Wonder how to strike up a conversation with a taciturn Northeasterner? Ask him or her to tell you the story of a town landmark—whether a one-room school, an old lighthouse, or a Revolutionary War battleground. Chances are you'll hear the tale as if it happened yesterday. In Northeast country, you'll find the foundations of a proud, strong America intact and little reason to wonder whether they will endure for generations to come.

Above: *Simplicity sometimes serves best and longest. The farmer who built this Saratoga County, New York, barn generations ago concentrated on sturdy construction without embellishments. These days, a coat of paint can't disguise the weary wood. The structure sags in some spots and timbers are failing in a couple of others. But the barn nevertheless wears its age gracefully.*

Opposite page: *Hiding among the leaves just a few feet from a state highway, the Upper Falls Bridge still carries traffic on a town road over the Black River in southern Vermont. Plain Yankee practicality probably helped to save this weathered old-timer and others you'll encounter on New England's back roads. Records on the subject are a trifle sketchy, but as far as anyone can tell, Peter Lasker built this bridge around 1858. He might be pleased that his handiwork is considered a historic landmark, but he'd undoubtedly be more interested to know the bridge is still doing its job.*

Above: *A frame chapel was torn down in 1877 to make way for the Old Union Methodist Church near Townsend, Delaware. But stones in the adjacent graveyard date to the congregation's earliest days. The oldest marker bears the name of one Sarah Fields, who died in 1799.* Left: *Eli Whitney's tombstone isn't the only impressive monument in the Grove Cemetery in New Haven, Connecticut. The inventor of the cotton gin shares the tract with such other notables as lexicographer Noah Webster and vulcanized rubber inventor Charles Goodyear. The cemetery dates to the 1790s, when 32 prominent New Haven citizens raised money to buy land for a Protestant burial ground. These practical founders saved future generations the grief of searching for their relations, organizing the cemetery into family plots. The cemetery is thought to be the first in America laid out in that fashion.*

Locals call Holy Trinity Church in Wilmington, Delaware, "Old Swedes Church," a nickname the old building wears comfortably after almost three centuries. Swedish immigrants settled Wilmington in 1638 and built the sturdy stone and brick church in 1698. The Dutch and then the English took over the village, but the settlers held onto their heritage. The church stands as it was built, and a loyal congregation still worships there.

Opposite page: *The Grist Mill, a reconstruction of the structures that once dotted New England, stands on the grounds of Old Wayside Inn in Sudbury, Massachusetts. The mill grinds flour used in the kitchens of the inn, which inspired Henry Wadsworth Longfellow's 1863 classic* Tales of a Wayside Inn. *In the poet's day, the hostel, the oldest in the country, already claimed a long history.*

Above: *When the Red Stone School stood on Red Stone Hill in Sterling, Massachusetts, a pupil named Mary had a lamb who followed her to class. Someone told this story to a young Harvard student named John Roulstone, who wrote the first 12 lines of the famous poem about Mary and her pet. Mary Josefa Hale finished the rhyme in 1830. Now, the restored school stands on the grounds of the Old Wayside Inn in Sudbury, Massachusetts.*

I praise the flower-barren fields the clouds the tall
Unanswering branches where the wind makes sullen noise

—Archibald MacLeish
"Immortal Autumn"

Peace long ago settled around this stone and timber cottage that the French general Lafayette commandeered for his quarters for the Battle of Brandywine, the Revolutionary War's largest one-day fight. Amid green fields drowsing in the summer sun, hardly a sign remains that thousands of patriots fought for their lives barely a stone's throw away. Now a 50-acre state park near Chad's Ford, west of Philadelphia, surrounds the cottage and George Washington's headquarters nearby.

Above: *Freshly painted barns, bulging silos, and lush pastures stand for prosperity in the farm country around Auburn, New York. Country roads thread past dairy operations where you'll undoubtedly see the area's grandes dames hard at work—that is, resting and grazing. Even for cows, they look uncommonly content.* Left: *Chemical fertilizers and motorized machinery spelled the beginning of the end for this old manure spreader. There probably was many a good season's work left in this old-timer, when a Pennsylvania farmer chose progress. Frozen by rust, the piece stands like a monument to the days when the only available growing aid might have been pungent, but it posed no threat to the environment.*

Right: *With its relatively tiny windows, the 1630s Hoxie House, the oldest on Cape Cod, Massachusetts, seems to have been built to keep out the harsh New World. The house, furnished in the spare style of those first settlers, stands with other historic buildings along Shawme Pond in Sandwich, the oldest town on the Cape. Early settlers built the pond to power nearby Dexter Mill, where visitors gather to watch demonstrations of old-time milling techniques.*

Left: *Rockers beckon on the porch of a country inn in Camden, Maine. Generations of vacationers have summered in this village on the coast, which calls itself the "place where the mountains meet the sea." The town now bustles with shops and restaurants, but nothing has managed to replace front-porch sitting as a revered summer pastime.* Opposite page: *Weathered stones mark graves at Gettysburg National Military Park. It was on this Pennsylvania battlefield—on July 1, 2, and 3, 1863—that Union General George Meade and his troops fought valiantly against Robert E. Lee's greatest northern invasion. More than 51,000 soldiers, on both sides, were killed, wounded, or missing. Even more than a century later, the tragedy of the conflict and the small monuments lined up in neat rows bring tears to visitors' eyes.*

Over a lost orchard I have strayed
In March when down the wooded ravine
The behemoth wind bellowed to the glade
By the sky-blue water before the rushes were green.
While yet the acorn cups crushed under feet
Against the moss mould, yellow as smoke;
And the lanterns of wild cucumbers quenched by sleet,
And gusts of winter hung by the leafless oak;

—Edgar Lee Masters
"The Lost Orchard"

Opposite page: *A cathedral of greenery arches over a rough road through western Pennsylvania's Allegheny National Forest. The preserve safeguards more than half a million acres of dense woodlands, where deer and black bears roam undisturbed and streams teem with trout and bass. When camping or hiking in remote parts of the forest, you're seeing the countryside much as the first settlers did.*

Above: *Twice rebuilt and now showing its age, the Waterloo Bridge has carried traffic on New Hampshire's Route 103 for more than 150 years. Once 400 covered bridges served travelers in the state. This old-timer, another down the road, and around 50 others are still doing their jobs. Fires, floods, and a demand for progress claimed most of the rest.*

There's no such thing as rushing into town for an Amish farmer in Pennsylvania's Dutch Country. As long as the mules plod steadily forward, he's happy to go at the pace that the animals choose. The "English" (the Amish term for outsiders) who visit this region had better be content to take their time. No matter how fast your car will travel, you'll probably travel at horse-and-buggy speed, too.

Above: *No glory or riches for the Green Mountain Boys'
leader. After the Revolution, Ethan Allen returned to this rustic cabin, now part of a historic site in Burlington, Vermont.
Nearby, stands a re-creation of the tavern where Allen and
his followers plotted the taking of Fort Ticonderoga. The
scrappy band declared independence not just from Britain but
from neighboring colonies as well, and Vermont at first was
excluded from membership in the original 13 colonies. Left:
The inventive, ever practical Shakers came up with the notion
of selling seeds in packets. The sales helped support Hancock
Shaker Village near Pittsfield, Massachusetts. Members be-
lieved in communal living, equality of the sexes, and
celibacy—a practice that didn't further the group's future.*

Above: *Generations of youngsters in Hebron, Connecticut, attended the one-room school on Burrows Hill Road before it closed in 1911. A neighbor whose father and grandfather studied there carefully looked after the old building. Preservationists restoring the school found three rows of rough-lumber desks standing ready as if children might return at any moment. A massive teacher's desk stands at the front of the room. Determined to build a desk fitting for the task of teaching all grades in the cramped quarters, craftsmen fashioned the desk where it still stands; it's too big to fit through the door. Left: Stiff-backed wooden desks fixed in neat rows set a disciplined tone in this schoolroom at Canterbury Shaker Village in New Hampshire. Members of the sect founded the 4,000 acre community in the country's early days. Of the original 100 buildings, 22 survive.*

Springfield, Vermont, sprouted along a 1700s military road that connected the Connecticut River Valley and Lake Champlain. In 1785 some of the earliest settlers pitched in to begin building the Eureka Schoolhouse. The old school, moved to its present site and restored in recent years, is the state's oldest surviving public building, a fitting tribute considering early Vermonters' regard for education.

Above: *Weather vanes were more than decoration on early American farms. But it didn't take long for the practical instrument to become one more expression of Yankee individuality. Often, they depicted winged creatures—eagles or common roosters. On duty in the Berkshires, this fellow may not be as graceful, but he tells which way the wind is blowing just as reliably.* Right: *The farmer who once took such pride in this barn comes no more. It stands as a legacy of another time on lands now part of the Delaware Water Gap National Recreation Area. Canoeists and hikers flock to the preserve, which claims 40 miles of the Delaware River Valley on the Pennsylvania–New Jersey state line, much of it onetime farmland.*

Farmland still rolls across much of New York state and cows far outnumber people in some counties. A jaunty dairy barn promises refuge from the coming storm in Dutchess County. Farmers first chose red for barns and other outbuildings because they had little choice. The color was inexpensive and plentiful.

Above: *Despite the jaunty red trim, this bridge on Route 119 crossing the Ashuelot River in southwest New Hampshire has worked hard for most of its long life. Built in 1864 on the sturdy lattice support system known as a thoroughly American design, the span shouldered loads of wood on their way to fuel the engines of the Ashuelot Railroad. Now the bridge holds a spot on the National Register of Historic Places.*

Opposite page: *The Erbs Bridge over Hammer Creek in Lancaster, Pennsylvania, takes its name from its builder, Samuel Erbs. Thirty-one covered bridges dot the county and residents proudly call their home "The Covered Bridge Capital of the World." No one wants to sound boastful. It's more a strong statement about the area's deep regard for its heritage.*

Bunker Hill School—standing on the grounds surrounding the Old Red Mill in Clinton, New Jersey—finally is getting the attention it deserves. Constructed in 1861 in Alexandria, New Jersey, the tiny building quartered children attending class until 1920. Before the Clinton Historical Society reclaimed the neglected structure in 1974 and moved it to its present site, the school had served as a chicken coop and a pigsty.

Above and left: *The Old Red Mill, a Clinton, New Jersey, landmark, qualifies as a structural jack-of-all-trades. The four-story mill started out processing wool around 1810. By about 1830, it was a grist mill. In later years, talc, graphite, and plaster were milled in the cavernous building. During its long life, the mill also pumped water for Clinton's fire hydrants and generated the city's first electrical power. Comfortably retired, the mill now serves as the centerpiece for a 10-acre park.*

Silos and storage tanks are the closest things to skyscrapers you'll see towering over dairy country in New York state. Even the biggest, busiest operations rest easily on the land. Those who live among the region's neat-as-a-pin, prosperous farms and rolling pastures cherish the uncluttered skyline.

Up from the meadows rich with corn,
Clear in the cool September morn.

—John Greenleaf Whittier
"Barbara Frietchie" [1864]

Left: Long-ago builders invested untold hours in the gathering and careful piecing of stones for this Lancaster, Pennsylvania, barn. No one wondered whether the effort was worth the result or considered constructing an easier to build, but flimsier, structure. A sturdy barn was a point of pride and a legacy for future generations. Below: The corn store looks even more plentiful when you consider the corn was grown and harvested without the help of motorized machinery on an Amish-owned farm near Lancaster, Pennsylvania. As part of their devotion to simplicity and manual work, the Amish use horse-drawn equipment. Their boxy farmhouses—roomy to accommodate several generations under one roof and painted white because other colors might express vanity—dot the countryside around Lancaster.

Left: *Once this historic railroad station at Chester, Vermont, bustled with comings and goings. As the polished tracks imply, trains still pull in regularly to this town on the Williams River in southern Vermont. But the station's no longer one of the most exciting places in town. Visitors climb aboard the Green Mountain Flyer, an excursion train that makes leisurely trips between Chester and Bellows Falls, a mill town on the Connecticut River.*

Right: *Youngsters once dreamed of places these tracks might lead and of boarding the trains that rocketed past their New England farms, whistles wailing in the night. This old trestle carries mostly trains loaded with freight these days. When television transports watchers in an instant, no one spends much time wondering where the tracks go. It's a shame, really, because no place could be as exciting as those imagination-conjured destinations.*

The screen door slaps companionably behind you on the way into this general store in Hubbarton, Vermont. You can buy just about everything you need, including sharp Vermont cheddar, some of the finest cheese made anywhere. But don't just rush off. The soda's ice-cold, and everyone takes a moment to reflect on the weather, a source of consternation statewide. You won't find shiny carts or automatic doors here, but if you buy more than an armload, someone's always more than happy to give you a hand.

Once this weathered wooden shop in Delaware served as headquarters for the most important man in town—the blacksmith. In pre-automobile America, nothing much happened without this craftsman's help. Folks depended on him for everything from the delicate job of shoeing their horses to repairing prized iron kettles.

Left: *Farm buildings settle into mountain country around the village of Woodstock in eastern Vermont— steadfast connections to the area's roots and reminders to vacationers who flock here that there's still work to be done. The Green Mountain State does justice to its name, remaining one of the country's most rural. Present-day Vermonters guard that rural character as vigilantly as their forebears fought for liberty. Above: A hay rake and other horse-drawn equipment still help out in gathering the harvest at Longstreet Farm in Monmouth County, New Jersey. After the cutting, the farmer bouncing along in this contraption rakes the hay into piles. The Longstreets (Americanized from the Dutch* Longstraat) *bought their first parcels of land around 1700, and a member of the family lived on the property until the 1970s.*

Opposite page: *Some say 1800s builders favored covered bridges because they resembled barns. Fooled into thinking they were headed home, horses and cattle that might have been spooked by rushing water crossed without a fuss. More likely, roofs like the one on the Albany Bridge over New Hampshire's Swift River protected the structure from the wind and water, as well as the builders from the job of replacing the bridge anytime too soon.*

Above: *The time when covered bridges fell to the demands for progress for its own sake thankfully has passed. State money helped spruce up the Henry Covered Bridge, an 1840 beauty that crosses the Walloomsac River in Bennington, Vermont. On surrounding slopes, Ethan Allen mustered his Green Mountain Boys for the fight against the Crown.*

Opposite page: *Some of the oldest barns, such as this stalwart in Vermont, stand unpainted. Old-time drummers traveled in wagons, brightly painted and new-looking on one side and unpainted and worse for the wear on the other. This was a testimony, these smooth-talkers told farmers, to the more-than-cosmetic benefits of a fresh coat. Truth be told, primitive paints that looked so pretty going on might have sealed in moisture and ultimately hastened the wood's demise.*

Right: *Dust settles finally on a hard-working gravel road and sunset casts the New York countryside in gold—a reward for the day's work done. The evening's peace is a gift in farm country, a respite to be savored if only for a moment. The fading light draws folks onto farmhouse porches and into yards, studying the sky for hints of what tomorrow will bring.*

Above: *Painstakingly carved Grecian urns line up along the palisade fence around the Old First Church in Bennington, Vermont. The early 19th-century builders prized simplicity, but they added touches that made their work unique. Poet Robert Frost rests in the church's cemetery.* Left: *The bell cradled in the steeple of the First Congregational Church in Windham, Connecticut, has rung a faithful congregation to service every Sunday since the church was built in 1886. One strong person or several youngsters pull the stout bell cords about 10:20 a.m., fair warning to any late sleepers that services are to begin in 10 minutes. The congregation looks forward to celebrating its 300th anniversary in the year 2000, and the pastor's confident the bell will ring for that service, too.*

✠ ✠

An early 1800s congregation invested $6,000 in the construction of the United Church of Acworth, New Hampshire, a princely sum in the days when the city hall was built for a total of $325. Dedicated in 1821, the handsome building, with its wedding-cake fancy steeple, offered scant worldly comforts to winter worshipers, however. Two fireplaces hardly heated the interior. Until 1830, members, fearful of fire, refused to install a stove. Men shivered and ladies re-sorted to cast-iron foot warmers heated next door.

The turbulent Browns River turned the machinery that ground flour at the Old Red Mill in Jericho, Vermont. Shut down since the turn of the century, the 1856 mill survives as a museum. Early New Englanders wasted no time harnessing the force of the region's rushing streams. Mills, large and small, sprang up on the banks of almost every river. Roads made their way to the water and towns grew up in the mills' shadows.

Brine and hints of yesterday's catch flavor the air, and salt-laced Atlantic winds season every surface in Menemsha, a seafaring village that is part of the town of Chilmark at the southwest corner of Martha's Vineyard off the Massachusetts coast. Vacationers flock to the island every summer, and the main business seems to be fun. But along this part of waterfront, the struggle for a share of the sea's bounty continues day after day. Traps pile up alongside fishing shacks waiting for the lobster trappers who will rise before dawn as they have for generations.

Left: *There's no practical reason to build covered bridges these days. Steel and other modern materials have no need for cover, and cars cross rivers without balking at the sight of flowing water. But a few bridge builders keep the craft alive for its own sake. Milton Graton built this youngster among Vermont's covered bridges in 1969 on the Ottauquechee River near Woodstock, Vermont—using the time-honored "lattice truss" design. His son, Arnold, carries on the tradition by building covered bridges. Below: On hot, sunny days, horses and drivers alike savored the cool shade provided by covered bridges such as this one, known as the Scott Bridge, in Townshend, Vermont. The respite lasted a good while, in this case, while wagons rolled through three sections of the bridge spanning a total 276 feet across the West River.*

Opposite page: *With its clock tower rising over Sugar Hill, New Hampshire, this schoolhouse speaks plainly about its builders even after almost two centuries. Early New Englanders gladly cast off the architectural embellishments of the Old World and constructed their homes and public buildings in spare, classic style. No effort was expended on gingerbread and nothing of the sort distracted from the building's function.*

Above: *Colonel Ebenezer Crafts and his band of 61 patriots might have marched the route this road now travels into East Craftsbury, Vermont. Crafts and his group founded East Craftsbury after the Revolution had been won. The colonel's son Samuel became one of the state's early governors. In autumn, it seems all roads in this northeastern part of the state thread through dazzling corridors of russet and glimmering amber.*

Opposite page: *All year, sightseers stop to see the cozy covered bridge that crosses Falls Brook in Kent Falls State Park in northwest Connecticut. But in autumn, the surrounding color-splashed bluffs steal the show. The brook tumbles over ledges of white marble, dropping 200 feet over the course of a mile. Newcomers who praise the region's unspoiled beauty are surprised to learn that this was once one of the most industrialized parts of the state. Manufacturing waned and time kindly has erased most traces of that era.*

Opposite page: *Shimmering Sunset Lake shoulders the rare pontoon bridge that leads into Brookfield, Vermont. Newcomers tend to make the odd crossing slowly and ask a lot of questions about the old bridge. But natives take the bouncy ride for granted. This one-time mill town manufactured pitchforks and an array of farm tools. Brookfield boasts an 1835 building that houses the local historical society and a proud display of Brookfield-made implements.* Below: *Along New England's country lanes, roadside stands brim with fall's bounty. Depending on the time of day, the farmer might help you pick a pumpkin for pie-making or point out one that most likely will last until you carve it into a jack-o'-lantern for Halloween. Sometimes, no one's available to mind the stand, but the merchant trusts that anyone who makes the journey will leave behind the asking price in the box provided.*

Above: *The sunset sky seems to mirror fiery fall hues that color the bluffs framing a Vermont farm. In autumn, the evening sky bears careful study. There's time for such reflection now that the summer's work is done. One of these days soon, the clouds will bring snow—but probably not today.*

Opposite page: *With a fresh coat of barn red, the Bridge on the Green, which has crossed the Batten Kill River in West Arlington, Vermont, since 1852, claims its share of attention even when autumn lights up the village. If this quiet town looks like something out of a Norman Rockwell painting, it is. The artist lived in the area for more than a decade and captured his surroundings in his* Saturday Evening Post *magazine covers. A nearby museum displays Rockwell's works.*

Above: *Flashing their autumn finery, the maples that shade the village green in Wells, Vermont, look almost gaudy next to graceful St. Paul's Episcopal Church. Founded in 1768 and named after a town in England, the village has remained a sleepy hamlet. Even though the church stands at the center of town, traffic noise or other commotion isn't likely to disturb Sunday services—or the peace of the week's other days, for that matter.*

Opposite page: *The century-old District 7 Schoolhouse no longer serves the children of Warren, Vermont, a village of 1,000 in the center of the state. These days, classes meet in a new modern building. But no one would think of wasting a structure with such a proud past. Gussied up in fresh paint and bright trim, the old building now shelters the library and town clerk's office.*

Right: *The tall ships long ago disappeared from New London's harbor, one of the deepest along the Connecticut shore, but the Pequot Avenue Lighthouse continues to stand a lonely vigil. At one time, 80 whalers sailed out of New London, more than from any other port except New Bedford and Nantucket. Huge profits— $150,000 for one voyage alone—built grand mansions that still stand along New London's Whale Oil Row.*

Opposite page: *Winter works magic in New England. A February storm played fairy godmother to Merrick Brook in Scotland, Connecticut. Shimmering white cloaks stream banks that were forlorn winter gray just a day ago. Branches that were bare and shivering now gently cradle new snow, weaving a pattern of sparkling lace against the sky.* Left: *No snow slicks the Kingsley Covered Bridge, which crosses the Mill River near Clarendon in south-central Vermont. The dry deck, a boon for 20th-century drivers, probably annoyed 19th-century travelers. Farmers employed horse-drawn sleighs to take advantage of snow-covered roads for transporting heavy loads. Some communities hired laborers for the task of spreading and packing snow evenly on main roads, guaranteeing sleighs smooth passage—a job every bit as vital as modern snowplowing.*

Over the woodlands brown and bare,

Over the harvest-fields forsaken,

Silent, and soft, and slow

Descends the snow.

—Henry Wadsworth Longfellow
"Snow-Flakes"

Above: *This Monroe, New Hampshire, churchyard slumbers undisturbed in the alabaster silence of a New England January. Here, no prints mar the foot or more of snow likely to pile up by spring and peace seems frozen in place for the season. By midwinter, the region's white church spires and villages seem to meld with the snowy landscape, and the countryside spreads out as clean and expectant as new parchment.*

Opposite page: *In winter, the people who own summer cottages around placid Brant Lake within the boundaries of New York state's Adirondack Park long ago have returned to their city homes. During this season, it's easy to see why the congregation chose cheery red for the steeple and door of the village church. The preserve embraces six million acres of mountains and lake terrain, the country's largest park outside Alaska.*

I'll tell you how the Sun rose—

A Ribbon at a time—

The Steeples swam in

　　Amethyst—

—*Emily Dickinson*
"Complete Poems"

Dawn swathes a New England farmstead in frozen mist. Winter's a quiet time on the farm, and this is the kind of day best spent with the kettle singing on the stove and a fire blazing in the hearth. Plenty of chores—from bookkeeping to machinery repair—wait for that time of year when cold keeps everyone indoors. There's no need to be idle, but the work can proceed at a more leisurely pace—without the urgency of planting and harvesting.

This round barn stands at the center of the "City of Peace" in western Massachusetts. That's what the Hancock Shaker Village's founders called the community they began building in 1790. Dubbed "Shakers" because of the gyrations that were part of their worship services, these idealists prized simplicity and practicality. The round barn, built in 1826, qualifies as a masterpiece on both counts. One man standing at the center of the three-story structure could feed 54 cows at once. The village, active until 1960, has been preserved as a museum.

THE SOUTH

Massive oaks guard the drive leading to the grand old house, once the centerpiece of a plantation that sprawled across hundreds of fertile acres. The oak branches form an intricate fretwork against a pale blue sky, the same color as one of the satin gowns the 19th-century lady of the house might have worn or the decorations on the delicate porcelain that graced the mahogany dining table. Cool shade bathes the drive and splashes over the massive white columns guarding the portico. Gravel crunches and dust rises in smoky plumes as cars travel a drive that seems meant for graceful carriages. You park and walk the rest of the way, but somehow the oaks and their shade want you to linger, as if the wind rustling in their massive branches was whispering a story of what life was like here once, and it wants you to listen. It's the story of the Old South, and it's probably best told in the wind's breathy sighs and impressions that come of their own accord from places like this plantation.

The region you'll travel bears only a passing resemblance to the New South you now hear so much about: The towers of downtown Atlanta or Birmingham and their surrounding contingent of manicured suburbs;

Opposite page: *Like the fragrance of magnolia blossoms, the tranquility of a more gracious era settles on Houmas Plantation in Burnside, Louisiana, north of New Orleans. Colonel John Preston of South Carolina built the palatial house in 1840 and named it for the Native American tribe that once claimed the area.* Above: *Kentucky's Calumet Farm is one of horse racing's most prestigious stables. It has bred eight Kentucky Derby champions, including Triple Crown winners Whirlaway in 1941 and Citation in 1948.*

the neon-lit commercial commotion of Orlando or Memphis; or the sleek beachfront hotels that preside over Florida's coasts, for example. The places and people of this appeased, unbuttoned South may be overshadowed and outshouted by the newcomers, but, otherwise, they're just fine, thank you.

Mostly, you'll find these places along two-lane roads that lace the region like worn ribbons. As long as you're not in a hurry, these routes will take you to places where the South's heritage comes alive. You'll find spots where a down-home welcome awaits. They also lead to solitary locations where generations of inhabitants from Indian hunting parties to struggling homesteaders never left much of a mark. Farmlands and pine forests still claim much of the countryside and stretches of seashore have escaped developers. You still can find spots where sun-warmed waters rush against the sands and tough grasses and stubby trees carry on a lonely fight to hold onto dunes. Steep blacktop climbs into mountain country so rugged that only the hardiest pioneers settled there. Now, their slopes shelter wilderness almost untouched and a culture that hasn't changed much in generations.

Beyond this region's cities and posh resorts, life often travels at tractor pace. Sunday dinners of fried chicken or baked ham with the whole family gathered around the table never went out of fashion. Country roads seem built for meandering. You can't rush past meadows bobbing with wildflowers, places that almost beg you to stop for a closer

look. There are vintage covered bridges and mills grinding grain as they have for more than a century.

In these parts, folks cherish their families and their pasts—whether an album of treasured sepia-toned old photographs, a rough-hewn log cabin that an ancestor built, or the lovingly restored Colonial homes and shops of Williamsburg, Virginia. The South's historic sites mark triumphs and tragedies alike. Pioneer settlements stand carefully preserved, monuments rise over battlefields grown peaceful, and restored slave cabins huddle on the remains of an antebellum plantation.

Small towns—no prospects in sight for any sort of boom and that's fine with most folks—cheerfully go

In 1736, the founders of the Methodist faith, John and Charles Wesley, preached to soldiers and settlers at the site where Christ Church now stands on St. Simons Island, Georgia. Ruins of grand plantations dot the island.

about their business. If you rise with the roosters, you can join the old-timers who have been meeting every morning as long as anyone can remember for steaming mugs of coffee at the cafe on Main Street. It's nothing new to hear about the summer of '58 that was blazes hotter than this one or the year drought shriveled the crops altogether, but it puts things in perspective somehow.

In carefully tended fields and lush pastures, you'll see a deep reverence for the land. The roots of this kinship reach across generations and the sea to countries where common people had scant hopes for a tiny plot let alone a rich acreage. No investment in this precious, hard-won land is too great. In some parts, hulking John Deeres and International Harvesters stand almost as tall as modest farmhouses, a clear statement of priorities. Each spread—small family operations and sweeping estates alike—could tell its own story of determination and hard labor rewarded.

Beneath the no-nonsense practicality that comes with this territory runs a current of graciousness that is refreshing as a cool breeze on a muggy summer evening. Oh, if you find your way to the wide porch of some grand house, you might be offered a mint julep just like in the movies. But, somehow, old-fashioned Southern hospitality seems even more delightful in an everyday setting. A Georgia produce vendor tending a roadside stand brimming with peaches demands that you put back a piece of fruit because it sports a bruise so tiny you wouldn't have noticed it. She picks a better one herself and insists you take another without charge.

As historic Williamsburg, Virginia, blooms in spring, it's hard to imagine the revolutionary fervor that once charged this village like an electric current. Colonial America comes to life amid the village's restored homes and shops. "Colonists" in flowing skirts and tricorner hats walk the streets and crafters ply time-honored trades.

A driver of a battered pickup that's trying your patience on a winding Arkansas road pulls to the shoulder and good-naturedly waves you ahead. A jean-clad waitress urges you to make a third trip to that buffet brimming with hush puppies and deep-fried catfish. Be sure to try the bread pudding and don't worry that it's almost closing time. This graciousness goes beyond mere politeness to genuine caring, and a stranger can't help but feel welcome.

The perfume of magnolia blossoms, the taste of a ripe peach, or the welcoming wave of a stranger characterize the region's friendly, relaxed essence. These reflections come together like the pieces of a mosaic to form an overall image of the great South.

Above: *In the days before instantaneous communication took the mystery out of such things, six-foot letters emblazoned on a neighbor's barn told you whatever was advertised had to be a sight worth seeing or something you ought to buy. Farmers such as this one near Bryson City, North Carolina, never would have stood for billboards cluttering up their land. But they didn't mind accepting $1 a year or so for putting some empty space to good use.*

Opposite page: *In their wholesale and dry goods store in Wheeling, West Virginia, cigar-makers Aaron and Samuel Bloch came up with the notion of making packets of chewing tobacco from clippings cut from stogie wrappers. The brothers paid farmers willing to have Mail Pouch slogans painted on their farm buildings and the signs became so familiar along country roads, you have to wonder if they sold much tobacco.*

Fence rails hewn from American chestnut long outlived the builder of this West Virginia homestead. More chestnuts than almost any other kind of tree once flourished in surrounding forests, and pioneers prized the wood for its resistance to rot. When a state park took over the farm and surrounding lands in the 1970s, delighted crews discovered the log cabin almost intact underneath white siding.

Using a mule to plow the garden isn't a lost art in northwest Arkansas' Ozark Mountains. Paved roads didn't make their way into these remote hills until well into this century, and natives cling to old ways, preserving skills that have disappeared in other areas. Without searching too hard, you can find folks who know how to make lye soap, hand-stitch quilts, and fashion a sturdy sweeper out of broomcorn.

*T*he state of the crop in the surrounding farms alters the expression of the earth from week to week.

—Ralph Waldo Emerson
"Nature"

Opposite page: *Now, quiet shrouds Burnside Bridge on Antietam National Battlefield in Maryland, site of the bloodiest single-day battle in American history. By the time the shooting stopped on September 17, 1862, 23,000 men on both sides were killed, wounded, or missing. Union General G.B. McClellan had managed to stop Robert E. Lee, but at a terrible price.*

Above: *Spring dawns gently in rural West Virginia. This time of year the region's country roads travel past greening pastures and forests leafing out in delicate new growth. You have to drive slowly with the windows down to savor the warming breeze and the sweet aroma of waking earth.*

The hearth formed the heart of the pioneer home. Mother cooked in cast-iron pots over the open fire, careful that sparks didn't catch her flowing dress. Evenings, the family gathered around a cheerful blaze for warmth and to share the events of the day.

He drove past grey-shingled farm-houses in orchards, past hay-fields and groves of oak, past villages with white steeples rising sharply into the fading sky

—Edith Wharton
"The Age of Innocence"

⊱⊰

North Carolina's Nantahala National Forest now surrounds the Stewart Cabin, actually half the structure that James Archer "Arch" Stewart built on the banks of Big Santeetlah Creek sometime around 1879. The other half was torn down. Even at twice its size, the cabin must have been a tight fit for the Stewarts and eight of their children. The cabin stands protected in the forest, but the couple left a much greater legacy in this region of the South; hundreds of their descendants still live in this part of the state.

Above: *The simple Quaker-inspired facade suited the somber setting for this 19th-century house in Round Hill, Virginia, the home of the overseer for the county poor farm. Forty unfortunate souls once labored to work off their debts on the 500-acre spread. Sherman's troops burned the barn on their march to sea—an act that probably didn't cause much mourning, at least among the county's poorer folks. Buildings remain from those grim days, but the present owners have transformed the place into the Poor House Farm Bed and Breakfast.*

Opposite page: *The county poor farm's onetime cookhouse in Round Hill, Virginia, now holds one of the Poor House Farm Bed and Breakfast's favorite suites. Guests cozy up to the massive hearth where cooks once prepared meager meals for the workers.*

Opposite page: *Swathed in morning mist, Virginia's Westover Plantation looks like an apparition from another time. In a way, it is. William Byrd II built the grand Georgian in 1730, and it stands as one of the finest examples of that kingly style. The tulip poplar on the front lawn probably was planted around the time the house was built.*

Right: *Stately oaks trailing beards of gray moss stand like sentinels along the drive leading to Boone Hall Plantation in Charleston, South Carolina. Major John Boone, an Englishman, was among the nation's first settlers, claiming the property in the early days of the Colonies. The first floor of the grand house, a later restoration, is open for tours. Nine slave cabins (also open to visitors) huddle on the property—reminders of the terrible price paid for this wealth.*

Above: *Oak Alley Plantation presides over the banks of the Mississippi River between Baton Rouge and New Orleans. In the heyday of paddle wheelers and flat boats, river captains who traveled between the two cities looked for the plantation as a landmark that told them they were halfway to port. Twenty-eight spreading oaks form a canopy over the quarter-mile lane leading to the sprawling house, now open to the public for tours.*

Opposite page: *In this North Carolina house and surrounding farm, Carl Sandburg and his wife, Paula, found a place that met both their needs. The poet craved a peaceful setting where he could walk and contemplate undisturbed. Paula wanted to raise goats. Carl Sandburg lived here from 1945 until his death in 1967. The National Park Service now operates the farm as a National Historic Site.*

In 1865 the builders of this cozy stone schoolhouse in Maryland weren't anticipating any sort of population explosion. A larger building replaced the old school in 1910. Now the schoolhouse stands restored with desks and a potbellied stove in Seneca Creek State Park. Grade school classes who visit to sample 19th-century education never fail to be impressed by the difficulty of learning without enough books and paper to go around, let alone the comforts they take for granted.

Above: *Like lace trim for Kentucky's velvet pasturelands, fences painted snowy white outline the state's Bluegrass country. Farms in this region pamper some of the world's most valuable thoroughbreds. Horse owners insist painting the fences white, an area tradition that's expensive and time-consuming, isn't just for decoration. White paint makes the fences more visible—and less of a threat—to running horses.* Left: *Spiffy as a jockey's silks, this Kentucky horse farm shines with pride that comes from producing generations of winners. More than 400 of these manicured operations hold sway over the state's lush Bluegrass region. Here, thoroughbreds live like kings in barns as elegant as townhouses surrounded by pastures that look as carefully tended as golf-course greens.*

A faithful congregation dedicated the Williston, North Carolina, Methodist Church in the early years of the century. Originally, a taller spire towered over the small-frame church, but that was struck by lightning. The rebuilt, shorter steeple stretches toward heaven, but not so far as to tempt the elements.

Gravestones of soldiers who died in the service of their country march across the green lawns of Arlington National Cemetery. Appropriately, Arlington, once the estate of Confederate general Robert E. Lee and burial grounds for more than 200,000 fighting men and women, overlooks the city of Washington, D.C. Some historians believe the government located the cemetery on the estate as a punishment for the Lee family.

Opposite page: *A long-ago pioneer cleared the timber from a plot in Tennessee and then used the wood to build this barn. Generations later his handiwork still provides passable shelter. Chances are the homesteader didn't have any help splitting logs. The rough-hewn timbers still show the marks of his broad ax.* Right: *Florida's Everglades National Park provides a haven for the great blue heron and thousands of other creatures. The park protects more than a million acres of subtropical wilderness that covers much of the state's southern tip: pine forests, swamplands, and grassy marshes where noisy 20th-century life seldom penetrates.*

Nature speaks in symbols and in signs.

—John Greenleaf Whittier
"To Charles Sumner"

Above: *Tobacco leaves dry in a Maryland barn. The leafy plant is native to America, and early explorers who visited the New World were astonished to find the natives "drinking smoke." By the late 1600s, ships left the Colonies loaded with cured leaves that found eager buyers in England.*

Opposite page: *If you count wealth in bales of hay, this Arkansas farmer ranks as one of the county's richest men. The bales line up like deliberate temptations for passing youngsters. The soft golden straw seems made for scrambling over and bouncing on, neither of which fits the farmer's plan for his hard-earned harvest.*

✄ ✄

Opposite page: *Mist wafts around forested peaks in Great Smoky Mountains National Park, which sprawls for 800 square miles across western North Carolina and eastern Tennessee. The mountains, part of the timeworn Appalachian range, shelter verdant valleys called "coves" like this one in Tennessee.*

✄ ✄

Right: *Hard at work since 1830 on the Little Pigeon River, the Old Mill in Pigeon Forge, Tennessee, promises customers "the finest flours, meals, grits, and pancake mixes." You can buy the stone-ground products at the mill shop, and the Corn Flour restaurant next door uses the mill's goods for baking. The cooks gladly give credit for at least some of their success to the freshly ground flour.*

Above: *Eastern Tennessee settlers invented the cantilevered barn, like this beauty reconstructed in 1968 across from the Oliver cabin in Cades Cove, Tennessee. A barn this size could shelter an average family's livestock—two horses and two cows. Lofts overhead stored hay, corn fodder, and seed; the overhangs kept wagons and farm machinery dry.*

Opposite page: *John Oliver might be surprised that the cabin he built in Cades Cove, Tennessee, now part of Great Smoky Mountains National Park, still stands and is a matter of so much interest. Visitors can't help but marvel at the construction—rough logs from trees felled nearby, hewn with a broad ax notched at the corners, and mortared with mud. No pegs or nails of any kind help hold the structure together. Oliver's family owned the cabin until the National Park Service bought the property in 1934.*

Grass pushes through the gravel on this country lane meandering through Kentucky farmlands. No one knows for sure whether the builders left the hump in the roadbed to discourage traffic and potential speeders, but it certainly has that effect. Chances are you could park in the center of the road and enjoy a picnic in the adjacent field without hearing any complaints.

Before the afternoon passes, rain will tap the tin roof of this grizzled barn slumped along a country road in Tennessee. But grasses and weeds have overtaken the surrounding farm field and no hard-working machines are sheltered here. Passersby only can guess what became of the farmer who once cared for these fields.

Above: *In more patient times, a Virginia farmer stacked the stones for this wall one by one along the route that the Blue Ridge Parkway now follows. It's not a road built for rushing from place to place. The parkway meanders for almost 500 miles through the Blue Ridge Mountains at a top speed of 45 mph, past upland meadows and overlooks where you can pull off for sweeping views.*

Opposite page: *A weathered barn looks even more tired next to the emerald brilliance of early summer in North Carolina. After watching many a season come and go, the old-timer patiently tolerates the eager landscape. The year's work has just begun.*

Above and right: *"Old Humpback" or "Grandaddy Bridge," as the oldest bridge in Virginia is fondly known, spans Dunlop Creek near Covington. Built by a Mr. Venable in 1835, the bridge once was one of three within a mile. The other two are long gone. After more than a century and a half, this old-timer holds a place of honor in a small park but no longer carries traffic.*

⊰ ⊱

Old Fort Harrod State Park recreates the first pioneer settlement west of the Alleghenies in Danville, Kentucky. When the nation was still young, James Harrod and his company of 32 men built the stockade with formidable ten-foot walls. Harrod's town claimed its share of "firsts" on the western frontier—from the first resident doctor to the first flock of chickens.

Opposite page: *In the last century, "Uncle Ed" Mabry and his wife, "Boss," built this grist mill south of Roanoke, Virginia, confident it would serve local farmers and turn a tidy sum. After a stint as a sawmill and blacksmithy, the mill is grinding grain again. These days, travelers along the Blue Ridge Parkway stop just to watch the massive stones at work and happily snap up bags of fresh ground flour, somehow sure it will taste better than the supermarket variety.*

Above: *Sunlight and shadows play tag on the sturdy walls of a stone mill in Little Rock, Arkansas. With the stones painstakingly fitted, the mill was built along authentic lines in a town park. In the old days, the builders would have congratulated themselves on such a sturdy building—more likely than most to stand against flood and fire, the two threats that eventually claimed most 19th-century mills.*

❈ ❈

Left: *Some claim that this pint-sized chapel in West Virginia is the world's smallest church. But the builders had more than an oddity in mind. Passersby are welcome to stop and offer a private prayer. The local 4-H Club carefully tends to The Little Church so it's ready for worshipers.*
Above: *A cherub forlornly keeps watch over the tombs crowded into an old New Orleans cemetery. Mourners are not able to bury their dead underground because of the high water table, so while born of necessity, these ornately decorated, massive aboveground chambers became monuments of esteem.*

*The oldest marker that is still legible in the graveyard of
Christ Episcopal Church in a historic area of Cambridge,
Maryland, dates to 1727. The congregation was established
in 1692, so some of the stones may well be older. In one
sense it doesn't matter that some of the stones have worn
smooth over the decades; the church still stands as a tribute
to the determination of its earliest members.*

Left: *Once an attendant at this Georgia gas station would have rushed out to fill your car with premium fuel and clean the windshield, dusty from a long trip on country roads. These days, since the building of the interstate, not much traffic passes this way. It's just as well, the tangle of blooms seems to say.* Above: *Lest diners accustomed to tinned, store-bought coffee or whirring electric gizmos wonder what the name is all about, this old-time grinder graces a post outside the Coffee Mill restaurant in Harper's Ferry, West Virginia. There was no such thing as "instant" in those days, when it took muscle power to crush the beans and a good long while to boil the brew.*

*Years of hard use and battling the weather give a pickup
character that a newer model cannot match. A comfortable
impression has worn into the driver's seat and there's a spot
rubbed shiny on the window ledge for the driver's elbow. The
engine's knocks and sputters have become as familiar as the
grumblings of an old friend.*

⊰ ⊱

Opposite page: *The first chills of autumn weave spicy oranges, bright russets, and threads of flashing gold across bluffs that rise around Harper's Ferry, West Virginia. By October, a beguiling crazy quilt of colors spreads over the hills. Hardly anyone can resist a closer look at nature's handiwork and Sunday drives have become a fall tradition in these parts.*

⊰ ⊱

Above: *Trains once brought wealthy vacationers intrigued by the healing waters at Eureka Springs in northwest Arkansas' hill country. Now old-time locomotives chug through surrounding mountains on sightseeing trips, and the village's Victorian charm and hospitality refresh vacationers at least as much as the springs do.*
Left: *In 1884, the B&O Railroad built the Oakland, Maryland, station in grand style, befitting the wealthy vacationers who traveled to the area's resorts. Tourists, mostly of more moderate means, still travel to the area, but they come in cars. Thus, the Queen Anne-style station, one of the oldest in the country, stands shuttered. But, in the business district of Oakland, the Garrett County seat, Victorian-era buildings house busy shops and offices.*

THE MIDWEST

Neat rows of green cornstalks, planted along furrows clean as a barbershop shave, march across fields that are tabletop flat and stretch in every direction as far as the eye can see. Like a plump hen sitting contentedly on a nest, a boxy white-frame farmhouse, two stories tall with a wide porch across the front and a flag fluttering from a pole planted in the yard, keeps watch from the middle of the farmland. This is central Illinois, but it just as easily could be Indiana or Iowa or parts of Missouri or even southern Michigan. This is the image of the Midwest that springs most easily to mind, perhaps even for those who know the region. The image is accurate, but it's not nearly complete.

Beyond the farm fields there are the wild lands of northern Michigan and Wisconsin where moose and black bear roam and waterfalls plunge over jagged cliffs. Along the Great Lakes shores, lighthouses stand watch over waters as blue as ink and as treacherous as any sea. In Missouri's Ozarks, timeworn mountains shelter rushing streams and weathered mills. Amid all the painstaking cultivation across the region, patches of prairie as indomitable as the region's spirit stubbornly bloom.

By midsummer, traveling across some parts of the Midwest, you'll see mile after mile of lush fields—corn, wheat, soybeans—or rolling pastures, home to contented cattle or hogs. The sun sets the schedule here. During the growing season, you're ready to work

Opposite page: *Herefords munch their supper from a wooden trough. This breed of beef cattle came to this country in the mid-1800s from England.* Above: *Everyone travels at horse-and-buggy pace on auction day around Shipshewana in northern Indiana. The Amish faith forbids members to own cars, so the "plain people" load up their buggies for the weekly trip, hoping to sell pigs, chickens, tomatoes, and baked goods.*

when the first rays slant across the farmyard and you don't think of stopping until the sun drops below the horizon. One farmer's fond of saying he's careful to close the screen door gently as he leaves the house before dawn on spring mornings, so as not to wake the rooster.

When the weather's passable, he works. If the winter lingers, if it rains too much or too little, or fails to warm up or warms up too soon, he worries. Supper waits, so do social outings and inside work. Even with the help of state-of-the-art machinery, long days take their toll and the weary farmer drags into the house long after dark. No matter how pressing the chores, though, he'll put his own work aside to help a neighbor whether

The steeple of this white church rises like hands brought together in a prayer of gratitude over the Kansas prairie and neat bales of hay.

it's bringing over covered dishes when there's a new baby in the family or carrying on planting for someone who's hurt.

If you ask whether he would trade farming for some other way of life, he'd probably be angry at the very suggestion. If he can't master the land or weather, at least no man is master over him. The satisfaction of watching the cornstalks or lithe shafts of wheat grow makes up for the heartache of drought, or hail, or flooded fields.

You can set boundaries for the Midwest, but the region's character blurs at the edges. To the east, Ohio's white-painted villages recall New England and restaurants serve Yankee pot roast. In southern Missouri, where you'll find cotton fields and eerie swamplands, tastes turn to fried chicken and grits. In western Kansas, cattle ranches and oil wells claim the wind-blown high prairie and, if there's only one cafe in town, you can bet steak tops the menu.

Not too many generations ago, the Midwest represented the edge of the frontier. New groups of immigrants—German, Scandinavian, Swiss, Czech, and Dutch—bypassed the already crowded East and founded new communities at the country's center. Religious groups, feeling the same pressures back in the East that they had in the Old Country, came in search of isolation and freedom. They found both. In Ohio and communities scattered across the region, the Amish reject cars, electricity, and other 20th-century conveniences. Members, dressed in somber, hand-sewn clothes and broad-brimmed hats, work the land with horse-drawn equipment, travel in horse-drawn buggies,

and make much of what they need—from boldly patterned quilts to finely crafted oak furniture.

Most of their Midwestern neighbors don't pretend to understand the Amish. But respect bordering on awe greets the "plain people"—as the Amish call themselves—as well as their customs and handiwork. The admiration comes from an appreciation of hard work and fine craftsmanship, but it also springs from empathy. Most Midwesterners need only look back a couple of generations to find ancestors with Old Country ways struggling to survive.

Every inch of plowed grassland, every plot cleared of timber, and every rough-hewn cabin or tiny settlement represents a hard-fought battle. The rural Midwest never forgot this struggle and preserves marks of victory from one-room schools where pioneer chil-

Early in the growing season, this Kansas farm holds only promise. If the rain comes and doesn't stay too long; if the sun shines, but doesn't bake the tender plants; if a marauding storm doesn't roar in, that promise will be fulfilled.

dren studied to creaky covered bridges and a cabin where Abraham Lincoln once lived.

The Midwest's pioneers dreamed of developing prosperous farms. Today's sprawling operations, feeding the nation and the world, long ago surpassed these settlers' wildest visions. Towns built around grain elevators and stockyards have grown into teeming centers of finance and industry. But the region's foundation rests squarely on its rich farmlands. You'll find its spirit in barns, in farmhouse kitchens, in white-frame country churches, and in wild places. The Midwest is not just the center of the country, but its true heart.

Left: *The Hodgson Mill and others built along streams that rush through southern Missouri's Ozark Mountains once provided an important part of the region's livelihood. A dwindling number still hide among the ancient mountains, reminders of the days when few roads found their way into these hills and people depended almost completely on what could be made or bartered close to home. Below: Michigan apple blossoms sparkle in white, while offering just a hint of rose. The soil and climate along Lake Michigan are ripe for fruit orchards; along with apples, you can find groves of cherries, peaches, plums, and pears.*

Above: *Slogans like this one painted on a southeast Ohio barn aren't likely to drum up much business these days. Reading it, passersby are more likely to long for simpler times when advertising pitches were only as plentiful as barns, and you wouldn't encounter one unless you happened to drive by.* Right: *This is the most beautiful vista for the Iowa farmer. There are more than 100,000 farms in this state, taking up 90 percent of its land area. And leading the country in corn production is almost an annual event for Iowa.*

Opposite page: *The "Little Brown Church in the Vale" existed first in the imagination of the writer of the 19th-century hymn, who happened on a wooded spot as he traveled to see his bride-to-be. When he returned to the site near Nashua in northeast Iowa, he found that villagers—moved by his song—had built the church. The song was sung at the church's dedication in 1864. Since church officials started keeping track, more than 60,000 couples have exchanged marriage vows in the church.*

Right: *The coziness of a tiny chapel near Festina, Iowa, embraces worshipers. Grand cathedrals remind the faithful of the Almighty's power. As the builders hoped, this small stone church with its handful of pews somehow brings Him closer and encourages friendly chats.*

Left: *Dusk settles on a southern Michigan farmyard. In this tranquil setting, it's hard to remember that Detroit's factories are less than an hour away. Most of the barns that rise over the landscape in this part of the country have been painted red or white. But, if you look closely, you'll see no two are alike. Each uniquely reflects the builder's needs, skills, and heritage.* Above: *Even with an umbrella providing a patch of shade, it's a hot, dusty day's work in an Indiana bean field. This farmer will tell you his lot is much easier than his father's and grandfather's. He can't imagine anyone choosing an air-conditioned office over working the land.*

*S*ilently one by one, in the infinite meadows of heaven
Blossomed the lovely stars, the forget-me-nots of the angels.

—Henry Wadsworth Longfellow
"Evangeline" [1847]

At twilight, town lights blink on along the horizon in Iowa's level farm country. The long, hot, hard work is done for today, leaving a few moments to enjoy the cool evening breeze. It's also time to savor the fresh scent of the greening fields and the plucky wildflowers that bloom with no help or encouragement beside the carefully tended furrows.

Above: *There's a surprise in store for anyone who thinks of the Midwestern prairie as a flat, featureless expanse of grass. Left to its own devices, the prairie assembles a colorful display that puts most contrived gardens to shame. In remnants of these grasslands that still flourish in Iowa, Missouri, Kansas, and other Midwestern states, hundreds of species of plants thrive side by side. Left: Prairie, with hardly a tree in sight, stretched as far as the early settlers of western Kansas could see. These inventive pioneers used sheets of tough sod to build shelters and fashioned fence posts from solid rock. These "rock posts" still line up across the countryside, monuments to determination and ingenuity.*

An early riser surveys an Iowa farm-yard. If you've ever seen a rooster strut, you can tell who really rules the roost. Farming ranks as the No. 1 occupation across this gently rolling, fertile land. When you measure riches in hens, hogs, cattle, and other farm animals, Iowa stands among the wealthiest states in the nation.

Above: *On the farm, only a fool wastes a moment of a fine day. The farmer certainly doesn't take good weather for granted. He works from dawn to dusk as if, after today, the sun might never shine again. His family knows better than to ask when he'll be done.*

Opposite page: *At dawn, the promise of a new day gleams as brightly as the freshly-painted barn on a Wisconsin farm. No one wastes a day like this one in farm country. Before the sun's up, you take a moment to sip steaming coffee and make plans for all that can be done before twilight—and in the days to come before winter blows in again from the north.*

Opposite page: *Tom and Sarah Lincoln lived in this simple cabin in Charleston, Illinois, when their son Abraham was elected to the nation's highest office; the president-elect made sure to visit before leaving for Washington. Restored as a state historic site, the cabin looks much like it did when the Lincolns lived here. Visitors can't help but reflect on how much of his strength and wisdom Lincoln drew from this humble home.*

Above: *A scruffy lichen aptly known as "Old Man's Beard" cloaks grave markers on Cemetery Island, one of 200 wilderness islands in Lake Superior that are part of Michigan's Isle Royale National Park. The graves belong to copper miners buried here in the 1800s. The remote islands' mineral deposits have attracted miners for thousands of years.*

Black-eyed Susans turn their happy faces to the sun in a Kansas farm field. Cheerful and pretty as yellow Easter bonnets, these hardy flowers dot remnants of the prairie that are their home. But, given half a chance, they will bloom almost anywhere from roadside ditches to untended fields.

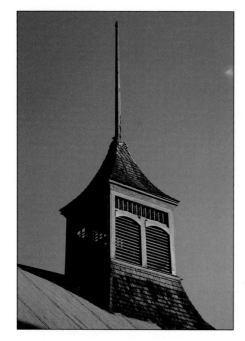

Above and right: *Swedish immigrants settled Lund in Pierce County, Wisconsin, near the Minnesota state line. A proud building in its day, this school symbolized the community's hopes for their children and life in the New World. The school, dedicated in 1887, served well until the 1950s when it was closed for lack of students. Now black-eyed Susans play in the overgrown schoolyard.*

Above: *A rural Wisconsin road fits nicely into the crook of a rocky outcropping. Eons ago, retreating glaciers and cascading meltwater carved quirky formations across this region. Residents take pride in these natural sculptures and natives—from road builders to farmers—long ago learned to work around them.*

Opposite page: *Winds roar across the Kansas prairie like a skyborne ocean, sometimes washing gently over wide-open landscape and at other times pounding everything in their path. Windmills spin over the state's farms and ranches, determined to catch at least some of that force. The energy created can pump water or drive a generator.*

Somewhere around 14 covered bridges once hid amid the cornfields of Madison County, Iowa. Fire, floods, and ice jams already had claimed more than half of those, when locals moved to save the surviving spans. Opposite page: *The Imes Bridge has carried traffic since 1870.* Above: *The Cutler-Donahoe Bridge was built the following year.* A sign on another of the Madison County bridges warned that anyone who crossed at faster than a walk could be fined $50.

Left and below: *The Hogback Bridge, a rare flat-top design built in 1854, crosses the North River in Madison County, one of more than a half-dozen covered spans that survive in this part of central Iowa. No one was too surprised when the bridges inspired a best-selling romantic novel. Old-timers joke that these are "kissing bridges" and courting couples look forward to crossing spans long enough for a private hug and a squeeze as well.*

Opposite page: *Summer sun glints off a whitewashed barn, keeping the interior relatively cool. On bright days like this, though, the haven is wasted. The farmer will work in the fields until the last of the light has faded from the sky, and probably well into the gloaming.*

Opposite page: *In 1864, William Weber built the five-story Dells Mill entirely of wood—even the gears—on Bridge Creek near Augusta in western Wisconsin. Visitors marvel as the vintage machinery grinds grains as it did in the last century. Exhibits tell the story of the age of water power. A town grew up around the mill with all the makings of 19th-century prosperity including a cooper to make wagons and wheels, a blacksmith, and a boarding house. Forward-thinking citizens built the Dells School (above) in 1866. The town's hopes faded when the railroad took another route soon after, but classes continued to meet in the school until the 1960s.*

Left: *The early 1900s come to life among the more than 30 historic buildings in Billie Creek Village in western Indiana's Parke County. The red one-room schoolhouse has been restored to look as if class is about to begin soon. You'll also find a black-smith, a potter, a broom-maker, a weaver, and other crafters hard at work plying their old-time skills in the village.*

Opposite page: *This brightly painted red barn stands against a blue sky as a testament to the rewards of hard work and the Midwest's fertile, black loam. Some of the most successful farms in the world flourish in this region.*

Opposite page: *Flickers of fall colors brighten the forests around this Wisconsin church. Traveling past on a weekday, you might wonder whether there are enough worshipers in this woodsy region to fill the pews. But on Sundays, the congregation comes from miles around. In this country, folks value their solitude enough that they don't mind and actually enjoy a bit of a drive.*

Right: *Built in a style simple and straightforward, this frame church near Galena nestles in northwestern Illinois' rolling hill country near the Iowa border. In these parts, churches still serve as centers for the surrounding farming community, and worshipers wouldn't think of missing Sunday services.*

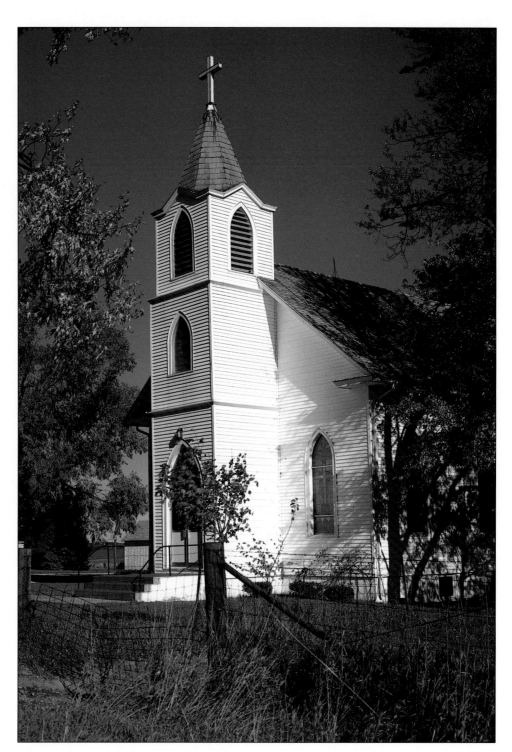

1906
BEESON
FRANKFORT CONSTRUCTION COMPANY - BUILDER
Moved to Billie Creek Village in 1980

More than 30 covered bridges tuck into the hilly, stream-laced terrain of western Indiana's Parke County, which proudly calls itself the "Covered Bridge Capital of the Midwest." Natives of this rural county aren't sure how so many of the rustic bridges, some dating to before the Civil War, survived. The whole county celebrates the landmarks with an annual covered bridge tour each fall. A map helps visitors find the Harry Evans Bridge (opposite page), *built in 1908, and the Beeson Bridge, a 1906 beauty* (above).

Under the cooling shadow of a stately elm

Close sat I by a goodly river's side,

Where gliding streams the rocks did overwhelm,

A lonely place, with pleasures dignified.

I once that loved the shady woods so well,

Now thought the rivers did the trees excel,

And if the sun would ever shine, there would I dwell.

—Anne Bradstreet
"Contemplations"

In the village of Munising on the north shore of Michigan's Upper Peninsula, a waterfall tumbles toward Lake Superior. Wilderness still claims much of the "UP," as Michiganders call the Upper Peninsula. Natives of this rugged country take such sights pretty much for granted. A half-dozen falls cascade around this harbor town, and there are more than 150 across the UP.

Left: *This lighthouse stead-fastly stands watch on the shores of Michigan's Isle Royale, rising from the cobalt waters of Lake Superior 50 miles north of the state's Upper Peninsula. Moose and timber wolves flourish in the lush forests of this island, the largest in an archipelago of 200 wilderness gems protected within a national park. Visitors who want to sample the soli-tude must come by ferry or sea plane.*

Right: *A handsome buck strikes a wary pose, his tawny coat blending with the mellow gold of an early autumn field. In many areas of the Midwest, his animal predators long ago have disappeared. Speeding automobiles and sprawling sub-divisions have become his greatest enemies.*

Above: *Shiny black buggies clip-clop along a country road leading to the tiny hamlet of Charm in north-central Ohio's Holmes County, where one of the country's largest Amish communities thrives. The sect, which shares roots with the Mennonite faith, forbids the ownership of cars and members live without electricity. More buggies than cars travel on some Holmes County roads and automobile drivers soon learn the pleasures of traveling at a slower pace.*

Opposite page: *Generations ago a farmer gave up on this Midwestern homestead. The battered buildings look even more forlorn against the green promise of the landscape. Many prospered in this lush farm country, but hard years—drought, plummeting crop prices, and more—exacted a heavy toll.*

The Mansfield Mill—a Parke County, Indiana, landmark—looks precarious towering over the riverbanks, but it's still grinding grain after more than 150 years. By way of qualification, Parke County history buffs will tell you the milling machinery is "only" a little more than 100 years old.

Falling Spring Mill tucks into the crook of a limestone bluff in Missouri. An ingenious design uses water from the overhead limestone to turn the creaky wheel. Nineteenth-century settlers loathed wasting the power of the Show-Me State's rushing streams and bubbling springs.

A sea of wheat washes past farm buildings on the Midwest prairie. Turn in any direction and you'll see the golden waves rolling across the level landscape to the horizon. The changing surface flows with the wind, showing eddies and swirls with every passing breeze.

Where long the shadows of the wind had rolled,

Green wheat was yielding to the change assigned;

And as by some vast magic undivined

The world was turning slowly into gold.

—*Edwin Arlington Robinson*
"The Sheaves"

Right: *Flashing in the sun like spun gold, ripening wheat sways gently over a Kansas field. Once the bottom of a prehistoric sea, the Sunflower State harbors some of the world's most fertile soil. Kansas farmers make good use of this bounty, harvesting more wheat than any other state.*

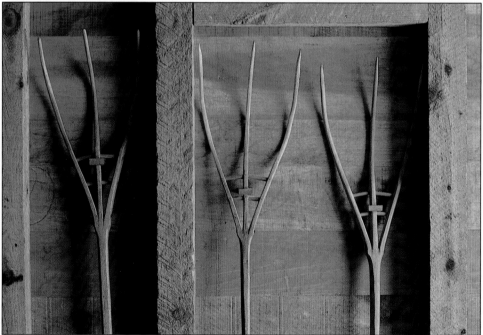

Left: *Wooden rakes, such as these used by long-ago stablehands, hang at Fort Scott National Historic Site in eastern Kansas. The compound's costumed soldiers and 20 buildings, including 11 originals, re-create mid-1800s military life. In those days, the fort served as a vital outpost on the fringes of the western frontier.*

Opposite page: *Nature moves quickly to reclaim an abandoned north woods homestead. Harsh winters and isolation had a way of dashing hopes that seemed reachable in the all-too-brief warmer months. The weathered cottage whispers a warning to passersby: Don't think life is easy in this willful country.*

Above: *An autumn moon smiles down on an Iowa farm, lighting the cornfields almost as brightly as day. Another bumper crop has been safely harvested and the year's work is done. In the Midwest, fall is a season for celebrating the land's bounty at church suppers and fall festivals of every sort.*

⊷══⊷ ⊶══⊶

Right: *On this windswept bluff top, a long-ago mourner made certain his loved ones never would lack for a view. Others who make the climb to these heights keep a respectful distance, and the fading stones stand undisturbed after more than a century.*

⊷══⊷ ⊶══⊶

Left: *Long ago, someone must have grieved deeply to erect this monument on the Illinois frontier. The stone served well, far outlasting any mourners for those buried in the neglected plot. Brambles close in as callously as the passing years, bound to erase any trace of these graves in another generation or so.*

Corn stubble—all that's left of another bumper crop—covers neat furrows in Illinois farm country. The husks and chaff will blanket the rich soil against marauding winds. In winter, you can see for miles in this level country. In summer, corn-stalks, taller than an adult and growing dense and lush as a jungle, form solid walls along country roads.

Opposite page: *The maples of Funks Grove in central Illinois rain butter-yellow leaves on the grounds of a tidy, white-frame church. A local farm taps the maples that flourish in this area and renders the sap into silky, sweet syrup.* Above: *Sugar maple boughs form a bright canopy over a little-traveled road through a Michigan forest. The trees look as if they begrudge the tunnel carved through their forest for this route. Unless a car passes soon, their leaves may bury the roadbed altogether.*

And then there crept
A little noiseless noise among the leaves,
Born of the very sigh that silences heaves.

—John Keats
"I Stood Tiptoe"

Left: *Forests lining railroad tracks traveling deep into Michigan's north woods blaze with autumn golds and crimsons. Wilderness reigns across much of the northern reaches of the Great Lakes State, so no one but an occasional train crew likely will see this spectacular show.*

Opposite page: *Once a lifeline to Michigan's north woods, this old-time steam locomotive now carries sightseers and train lovers. Planes speed you to your destination and cars travel when and where you want to go, but neither mode of transportation comes close to the allure of train travel—listening to the soothing rhythm of steel against steel or the whistle calling as the engine and its procession charge through the wilderness.*

Above: *In another time, a farmer took great pains building this barn, and once it may have been the envy of his neighbors. But with work to be done from sunup to sundown, no one has time to care much for it these days. Neglect exacts a slow toll, as if the old building patiently is trying to hold out until someone comes along to make repairs.* Left: *It would be a shame to tear down such painstaking handiwork. But there is no need, because the horses that call this stable home don't much care about the rafters overhead, and their master takes a few moments to check up on the spider's progress every morning.*

Maybe the farmer celebrated the day he put this old plow out to pasture, thinking new machinery would make life easier for them both. He might just as well have wondered, though, whether anything really would do the job as well, and if he might be back for his old helper.

I hear America singing, the varied carols I hear.

—Walt Whitman
"I Hear America Singing"

Above: *Farm buildings huddle after an unexpected snowstorm freezes central Illinois farm country. This morning, nothing's stirring outside in knee-deep drifts. It's a day for keeping the coffee pot on and going over last year's accounts. Thoughts turn to spring planting and hopes for next year.* Opposite page: *One of the Midwest's fickle February storms casts everything in its path in frozen crystal; only the airborne seem unperturbed. State-of-the-art transportation proves no match for such displays of winter's raw power, and the show is best appreciated from indoors, preferably beside a cozy fire.*

Opposite page: *No snow days for children who attended this one-room school in South Lyon, Michigan, west of Detroit's spreading suburbs. When the bell in the steeple clanged, youngsters, bundled so that only their eyes showed, crunched to class over frozen pathways. Nothing less than a blizzard would mean a day off.*

Above: *Snow sweeps across central Wisconsin, transforming woods into a fantasy of sparkling white, as the Black River winds toward the Mississippi. Bare branches become a delicate embroidery, and still waters a polished mirror. Winter stills the region's remote forests, and, in some years, no human footprint will mark the snow.*

Above: *Ice transforms a Wisconsin farm field into a glittering garden of delicate glass sculptures. Snow—from raging blizzards to nickel-size flakes that fall in wet dollops—blankets this boreal country again and again over the course of a winter. But occasionally, as if to demand the attention of those who take white landscape for granted, the season stages an almost-magical finale.*

Opposite page: *Lighthouses built to guide vessels navigating treacherous Great Lakes waters still stand guard along Michigan's shoreline of more than 1,000 miles. This fire-engine red station presides over the shore on Lake Michigan near Holland. In winter, you can ramble this stretch of shore undisturbed. In warmer months, anglers try their luck from the surrounding pier and swimmers and sunbathers crowd the beach.*

❊ ❊
THE WEST

A sky the startling blue of cornflowers arches over a frozen Wyoming plane glistening with last night's dusting of new snow. The white expanse dwarfs a herd of hundreds of elk foraging at the center. The snow-covered plane stretches to the base of mountains that rise like walls. The mountains loom enormous, but they really are miles away. Their jagged peaks rise more than a mile above the plane, but they still can't seem to touch the soaring sky.

The same sort of bright blue stretches over the sunbaked, rocky flats. Scrubby bushes and foliage in spiky clumps scatter across a landscape that seems empty except for a few dark specks tucked into a corner of the sky near the horizon. As the car seems to crawl toward the distant silhouettes, buildings begin to take shape. Even from far away, it's clear no one lives here. A saloon and a couple shacks that might have been houses stand abandoned, but not in a way that appears deliberate. People seem to have just moved on and forgotten this place. A door hangs on its hinges and tumbleweeds somersault across the road, as if they are delighted to have this place finally to themselves.

Above: *The prairie blushes scarlet on an abandoned North Dakota homestead, making this harsh country seem almost welcoming. Homesteaders were slow to find their way to these lands, yet some found success growing wheat and raising cattle.* Opposite page: *The old saloon in the ghost town of White Oaks, New Mexico, was still serving cold beer long after most of the other buildings in the burg were shuttered.*

In another part of this region, a centuries-old church with thick, cool adobe walls built in the Mediterranean style of the congregation's founders stands at the center of a garden as colorful as a fiesta. Inside, worshipers murmur prayers and chant soft refrains in Spanish. Members cherish the language and customs of their homeland, and pass these traditions onto their children.

This is the West, a region so grand that mile-high mountain ranges seem built to scale for the landscape. It's a land that's still so wild in parts that whole towns can stand abandoned and no one notices much or needs the space. The giant landscape swallows successes and miserable failures alike. It's too big to be a melting pot and an array of cultures flourish. Immigrants and Native Americans hold fast to their heritage, carrying on eons-old customs. Cities—Los Angeles, Denver, Seattle—sprawl across hundreds of square miles, but in this enormous country, so many more square miles remain unspoiled. Meander just minutes down the coast from L.A. and you can squish your toes in the tawny sands of a solitary beach and play tag alone with the frothy surf.

The West endures as the United States' last frontier and huge chunks of this territory remain not just untamed, but hardly touched. This vast land has both its beauties and contrasts. There are traditions older than this country and places where the preserved past seems young and raw compared to the established East.

The explorers' tales of the West set fire to imaginations of 19th-century Easterners who were very disenchanted with this country's long-settled, already-crowded regions. The stories appealed the most to those with the least hope—farmers eking a living from small, rocky plots and immigrants crowded into burgeoning cities. They dreamed of warm, rich lands, plentiful and as easy for the taking as ripe apples bowing the boughs of an orchard. In these visions, the difficulties

In the 1880s, the town of Calico, California, grew rich on silver mined from the multicolored rocks of the "calico" hills. A dip in silver prices started the town's decline and by the turn of the century Calico was more or less deserted.

of the journey across wilderness and mountains seemed no worse than those they endured every day.

The immense Western lands mocked these meager dreams. The landscape the homesteaders imagined paled next to the glorious reality they discovered as they moved westward—from the wildflower-studded prairie and broad rivers to the majestic Rockies. They braced for a long trip and difficulties on the trail, but nothing could have prepared them for the monthslong, agonizing journey that they faced or the crushing hardships that slammed their hopes along the way. The vast West cut even the most cocky down to size and taught the greatest dreamers that they might not be thinking big enough.

The land's rigors forged a prickly, barbed-wire toughness in survivors and encouraged boldness. Families bravely built homesteads so remote they traveled for most of a day to reach the next farm. Night fell with an eerie finality on these lonely spreads and winter closed in like a hungry predator. Adventurers laid claim to ranches that stretched over thousands of acres. Sinewy longhorns, tough and ornery, ruled this range. With the tenacity of unbroken stallions, these ranchers bucked fencing of the range and battled for water rights. Legacies of this fighting spirit still dot the landscape. In the shadows of the Rockies, prosperous Colorado farms thrive. Successful spreads in Arizona and New Mexico command thousands of acres.

The potential of the lush lands along the coast lured some settlers. You can see fulfillment of that promise in vineyards that stripe sun-washed California hillsides and citrus groves that bask in the gentle climate. Other fortune-seekers stampeded westward lusting after a share of the gold discovered glinting in mountain streams. Some struck it rich. Prosperous operations still sift gold from the Black Hills and other Western mines. Many more gave up the treasure hunt without so much as a single strike or when shallow veins petered out. Boom towns that sprang like weeds from the landscape went bust just as suddenly. The remains of these towns—ramshackle mine offices and abandoned shacks—bleach in the sun like buzzard-picked carcasses. Their weathered facades seem to whisper warnings of luck run out and hopes lost.

Oblivious to the rushes and booms and migrations, the West's natural wonders endure. Cliffs the rich red of a flaming sunset rise over the Arizona range. Hulking peaks wearing year-round cloaks of white across their massive shoulders tower over the landscape of Colorado and Wyoming like somber giants. The deserts of New Mexico dance with a carnival of blooms. Flashing like tossed diamonds, pristine waters hurtle through jagged Rocky Mountain canyons. On the coast, dark cliffs turn immutable faces to the pounding Pacific and centuries-old redwoods reign over forests.

These natural wonders stand side-by-side with the inspiring handiwork of the homesteaders, ranchers, and all types of adventurers who tamed pieces of this rough country. The West still captures those big dreams, busted hopes, and wild lands. Here is America's last frontier—a landscape more thrilling because it may never be conquered.

Wyoming, an Indian word that means "land of vast plains," still qualifies as cowboy country. Cattle and sheep graze on more than half of the state's lands.

Above: *Engineers made Lake Houston, but then nature swiftly assumed control. Lush greenery surrounds the quiet water, and cypress trees flourish in the shallows of the lake, a reservoir created when the San Jacinto River was dammed to provide water for the city of Houston, Texas. A rickety pier halfheartedly accommodates small craft, as if reluctant to see the water's placid surface disturbed.*

Opposite page: *The Spanish dubbed steep-sided plateaus that are common to the West "mesas," which means tables. Spring's hopeful, new green washes over broad Johnson Mesa in the northeast corner of New Mexico. The sky seems to loom just over the rooftop of this neglected abode.*

*T*here seemed to be nothing to see;
no fences, no creeks or trees, no hills or
fields. If there was a road, I could not
make it out in the faint starlight. There
was nothing but land: not a country at
all, but the material out of which
countries are made.

—Willa Cather
"My Ántonia"

✣ ✣

Around the turn of the century, it was a sign of changing times and encroaching civilization when the builder adorned Community Presbyterian Church in Lamoille, Nevada, with embellishments in the gothic style that was all the rage in the East. Locals call it "the Little Church of the Crossroads," because the town was where California-bound settlers decided whether to head for Los Angeles or San Francisco.

Above: *The Sauer-Beckmann Farm at Lyndon B. Johnson National Historical Park near Johnson City, Texas, illustrates to visitors life on an early 1900s Western farm. The Sauers raised 10 children in the modest farmhouse. One daughter grew up to be a midwife. She delivered President Lyndon Baines Johnson, who was born nearby.* Right: *Onions dry in the farm's smokehouse, a common means of preserving this vegetable in the days before refrigeration.*

An Oregon farmhouse presides over acres of sunny wheat, the state's leading crop. Beginning in 1830, thousands of homesteaders and fortune hunters followed the Oregon Trail, bound for the region's lush lands. Although the heavy traffic lapsed more than 100 years ago, ruts from wagon wheels still mark the trail route.

The Rocky Mountains rise over emerald pasturelands near Bozeman in southwest Montana. The Lewis and Clark expedition made the first forays into this sprawling, mountainous country and much of Montana remains little changed since those early days. Only three states—Texas, California, and Alaska—claim more area. Only two, Alaska and Wyoming, have fewer people.

Hardy blooms stage a fiesta of fiery red and sunny yellow around a remote track that winds through southern California's Tehachapi Mountains. As persistent as they are pretty, the tiny wildflowers sprout in the little-traveled road's center and blur its edges. Given time, they may reclaim the route altogether.

❋ ❋

A vineyard stripes a sunny hillside in California's fertile Napa Valley. Balmy days and cool nights pamper the vines and their fragile fruit. Vintners first recognized the area's potential in the 1860s. Today, more than 300 vineyards and 400 wineries flourish in the valley and surrounding areas.

Above: *Summer gentles North Dakota's vast prairies. In these warmer months, hope blossomed among homesteaders who dared to settle this remote country. Winter's killing cold and blizzards that rolled across the wide-open land like buzz saws tested the firmest resolve. No one remains to tell this lonesome homestead's tale.*

Opposite page: *A summer storm builds over the Sangre de Cristo Mountains in south-central Colorado, gathering force to descend on the farm country to the east. Natives have learned to weather fierce, fickle storms that roar down from the heights, bringing spectacular lightning and slashing rains in warmer months and burying everything in sight in winter.*

Above: *Officers quarters line up in neat ranks like soldiers on parade at Fort Davis, a garrison maintained from 1854 until 1891 on the Texas frontier. Even at such an outpost, while their troops squeezed into cramped barracks, officers lived a life to be envied. The fort has been restored as a National Historic Site. In the summer months, costumed "soldiers" again drill on the garrison grounds.*

Opposite page: *The 8th Infantry established Fort McKavett, now a state historic site, near Junction City, Texas, during the middle of the last century to keep watch over the uneasy frontier. A company of elite troops, called Dragoons, also were billeted here. The fort closed when hostilities between the settlers and the Comanches and Apaches eased.*

In 1879, miners with high hopes for prosperity named this New Mexico town White Oaks for the stand of trees that surrounded two local springs. Over the next 25 years, the town's mines produced millions of dollars worth of gold and silver. After the mines shut down, the population dwindled slowly, and now White Oaks is a ghost town. The school, once the pride of the community, closed without fanfare.

Right: *The congregation long ago abandoned this church along with the rest of Bodie, California. The onetime mining town, now a state historic site, boomed on gold and silver in the Sierra Nevada Mountains. In its heyday 7,000 people lived in Bodie. The town's luck ran out along with the miners'. The last residents left and the post office closed in the 1940s, leaving behind some 170 buildings. In the schoolroom* (below), *books piled on desks and lessons on the carefully written blackboards look as if the children might return at any moment.*

Opposite page: *General George Armstrong Custer and more than 200 of his cavalrymen were buried where they fell at the Battle of the Little Bighorn River in Montana. A national monument now marks the site. Custer's troops clashed with Sioux and Cheyenne warriors led by Chief Sitting Bull.*

Above: *The Southern Pacific Railroad once stopped at this neglected station at the edge of the desert not far from parched Death Valley in Lone Pine, California. Train travel in the late 1800s and early years of this century, while smoother and faster than the stagecoach, still could be an ordeal. The building, fine in its day, offered weary travelers a welcome oasis on this hot, dusty trip.*

❄ ❄

An open door announces a vacancy in this Wyoming outhouse along the route that the Oregon Trail once followed. Even today, there wouldn't be much worry over privacy in this remote region. At one time, such a facility represented the height of luxury for this rough country. The finest ranches might have had two outhouses—one for the men and one for the ladies.

❋ ❋

Right: *In a sometimes bloody, ultimately futile fight, ranchers battled against fencing of the range, insisting that their cattle needed freedom to roam in search of grazing lands. Homesteaders fought for the right to keep trampling, voracious herds off their land. In 1867, Lucien Smith filed a patent application for the barbed wire that eventually would end the days of the open range. Angry cattlemen decried the wire as "devil's rope."*

❋ ❋

Left: *Longhorn cattle once ruled the West. By age seven, the breed's horns might measure four to five feet. In the mid-1800s, 50 million longhorn thundered over the ranges of Texas and other Western states. Ranchers found the longhorns to be as tough as the land itself, thriving in harsh range conditions and surviving the long drives to market.*

Above: *No windows break the cool gloom in the Honey Run Covered Bridge in Butte County near Chico in northern California. The span, an engineering masterpiece in its day, no longer is a public thoroughfare, and no one takes much notice of it now. The traffic that encouraged the bridge's construction long ago found other routes.*

Opposite page: *Travelers once paid tolls to cross this 230-foot bridge across the crystalline Yuba River in northern California. The traffic—mostly gold and silver miners on their way to and from prosperous digs in the surrounding mountains—could well afford to pay. The builders thought it was only fair that these prospectors should help bear the costs of the construction.*

Like the character of the region, San Raphael in La Cueva in New Mexico's northeast corner blends Eastern U.S. and Spanish influences. The lonely old building, wearing its steeple like a stiffly starched collar, looks somehow out of place and uneasy perched on the incongruous landscape under a wide blue Western sky.

❊ ❊

Right: *The Spanish settled the village of Chimayo in New Mexico's Peppercorn Hills a century before the English arrived on the United States' East Coast. Residents hold fast to customs rooted in even older traditions. The Catholic church, the center of life in this sleepy hamlet, dates to 1814. The faithful make pilgrimages to the adjoining chapel, which believers say has been the site of miraculous cures.*

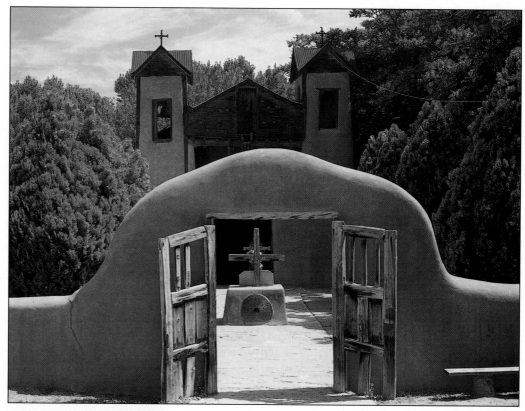

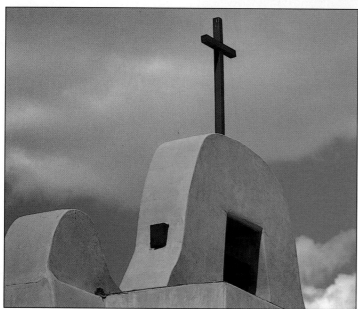

❊ ❊

Left: *A wooden cross crowns a historic New Mexico mission as an unadorned symbol of hope rising over the parched landscape. The Spanish priests who supervised building of these outposts of Christianity favored adobe construction and simple designs familiar to their followers. The adobe walls helped keep worshipers cool despite soaring summer temperatures.*

❋ ❋

Opposite page: *Clouds mound into peaks of their own hovering among the jagged summits of the Grand Tetons. The highest of the mountains in this range—Grand Teton itself—looms 7,000 feet above the Snake River Valley floor. When early 1800s explorers returned to the East with stories of this stunning mountain country, many skeptical city dwellers dismissed the reports as tall tales.*

❋ ❋

Above: *Small ranches, operations handed down through families for generations, still prosper in Colorado. Many of these spreads' founders chose land and hard work over dreams of gold or silver. Their descendants could testify that these ranchers are the ones who really struck it rich.* Left: *An older tractor rests in this Colorado field as if the rancher might return for it at any moment. You'll hear the farmer say the old equipment will go as soon as he has the time. But somehow it just doesn't get done. There's a part of him that can't bear to discard anything, suspecting there just might be a use for that old tractor someday.*

Above: *Four rivers flow into Tillamook Bay, Oregon—along U.S. Highway 1—and join the Pacific. Salmon throng the rivers during annual runs and the bay once supported a thriving commercial fishing industry. Waterlogged pilings recall those days. Now anglers flock to the area.*

Opposite page: *The Rockies rise in the distance beyond a farm near Boulder, Colorado. Even natives learn to never take for granted the magnificent views in this region. Mountains only claim about half the state's area. Ranches raise sheep and cattle, and farms grow corn and wheat in the fertile country that runs across the state's center.*

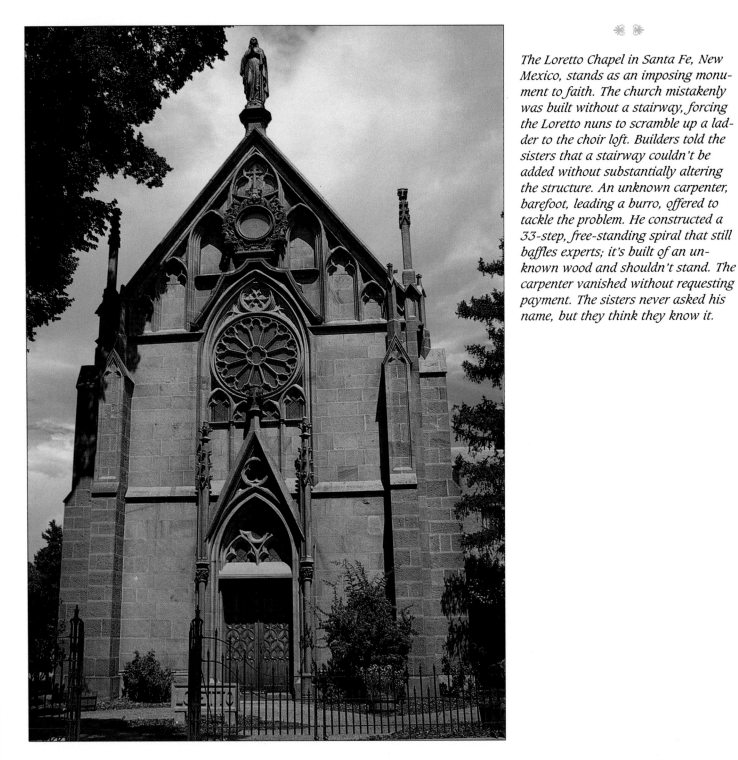

❅ ❅

The Loretto Chapel in Santa Fe, New Mexico, stands as an imposing monument to faith. The church mistakenly was built without a stairway, forcing the Loretto nuns to scramble up a ladder to the choir loft. Builders told the sisters that a stairway couldn't be added without substantially altering the structure. An unknown carpenter, barefoot, leading a burro, offered to tackle the problem. He constructed a 33-step, free-standing spiral that still baffles experts; it's built of an unknown wood and shouldn't stand. The carpenter vanished without requesting payment. The sisters never asked his name, but they think they know it.

Mormon settlers founded the town of Junction, Utah, in 1878
and built a log school at the base of a towering bluff that
came to be called Capitol Reef. At first, the school made do
with a sod roof. Shingles were added in 1912. Unlike so
many others on the frontier, this little community prospered.
The settlers planted orchards in the fertile soil, part of the
Fremont River Valley, and fruit trees flourished.

Opposite page: *Members of a tribe in Eklutna, Alaska, north of Anchorage, build colorful houses to stand on the graves of their loved ones, homes to be enjoyed in the afterlife. The designs of the "spirit houses" blend tribal beliefs and borrowings from the Russian Orthodox faith, a legacy of the largest state's first European settlers.*

Right: *The simple lines and ivory facade of this tiny church stands amid a carnival of foliage on Maui, one of Hawaii's larger islands. The contrast between the beliefs of 19th-century European missionaries and the colorful customs of the island's Polynesian inhabitants was striking. These days, the two cultures have found harmony and balance.*

Opposite page: *After more than a century, Pigeon Point Lighthouse still stands watch along the craggy California coast north of Santa Cruz. The 115-foot light tower holds the original Fresnel lens. The Pacific heaves and boils along this stretch of shore and waves crash around the windswept point. In earlier days, the tower tossed its brave beacon like a tenuous lifeline, the only help for ships making their way through the dark in angry seas.*

Above: *Settlers on the California coast built this one-room school in 1872 on the old Los Osos Valley Road in San Luis Obisbo County. Around the turn of the century, the blossoming area outgrew the old school and it fell into disrepair. Recently, the school was renovated and moved to a place of honor.*

Above: *This store still operates on a limited basis in Old Benton, California, a town that grew up around a silver mine in the 1850s. In better days, the Wells Fargo stage stopped at this site. An inn has been converted into an artist's gallery nearby. But otherwise the hoped-for tourist boom still seems a long way off.* Left: *Future jack-o'-lanterns grow plump on a Santa Paula, California, farm. The southern California climate pampers all types of crops and the growing season lasts for most of the year. California farm production tops all other states and the Golden State produces more than half of the nation's fruits, nuts, and vegetables.*

❋ ❋

This water tower in the northern California town of Yreka once fueled thirsty steam engines hauling timber cut from surrounding forested mountain country. The Blue Goose Railroad continues to make regular runs, but the cargo has changed. Sightseers board for three-hour trips that travel through the Shasta Valley, home to sprawling cattle ranches.

❋ ❋

$\mathcal{M}$ountains are earth's undecaying monuments.

—Nathaniel Hawthorne
"Sketches from Memory" [1868]

Ripening wheat, one of Washington state's leading crops, gilds the plains that sprawl beneath Mount Adams, a peak that soars to more than 12,000 feet in the Cascade Range. Glaciers cap the tallest peaks in the range—including Mount Rainier, which is 14,000 feet. The range rises like a wall down the state's eastern third, and wilderness still reigns in the surrounding rugged country.

Above: *Mountains frame a tumbledown Wyoming ranch languishing in the valley known as Jackson Hole, a level upland squeezed between the Grand Tetons and Gros Ventre Mountains. The nearby town of Jackson started as a fur-trading post. These days, skiers flock here, but the town still looks like a set from a cowboy movie. Left: Horses provide some of the most dependable transportation in wilder parts of the West. Ranchers admit, though, that they wouldn't give up their horses even if the animals weren't needed. Loping across the range on horseback, you can feel the freedom that brought settlers to this wide-open country in the first place.*

When autumn fires the surrounding forested hills, Douglas County Oregon's white-painted covered bridges can't hide amid the foliage. The Rochester Covered Bridge (above), *built in 1933, crosses the Calapooza River near Oakland. The Neal Lane Covered Bridge* (opposite page), *spanning the south part of Myrtle Creek, was built in 1929. These bridges may be newer than their counterparts back East, but they carry an ageless spirit of craftsmanship.*

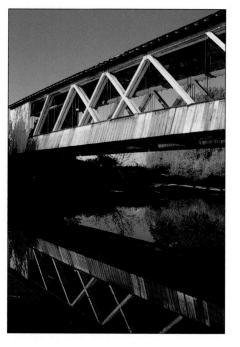

❊ ❊

Oregon builders favored covered bridges long after Easterners abandoned the old-time design in favor of sleek, steel spans. Wood from the area's great forest was plentiful, so the tried-and-true method made sense. All built in this century and one nearly 30 years ago, these covered bridges reside in Linn County west of the Cascade range. Built in 1947, the Bohemian Hall Bridge (left), travels 120 feet across Crabtree Creek. The Gilkey Bridge (above), mirrored in placid Thomas Creek, dates to 1939. The Shimanek Bridge (opposite page), also over Thomas Creek, was "just" built in 1966.

New Mexico calls itself "the Land of Enchantment," but the entire region casts a spell. Warm sunset hues wash over the land and color otherworldly rock sculptures. Under an arching blue sky, a hulking butte—carved by wind and ancient waters of terra-cotta-colored sandstone—soars over the New Mexico landscape.

In fall, Colorado aspens flash like the bits of gold 19th-century prospectors hoped to find in the state's rocky streams. It's an arduous trip on a mountain road to a mill built in the last century on the Crystal River. The mill was abandoned decades ago, and the surrounding area remains mostly primitive.

❈ ❈

Left: *When miners abandoned the town of Terlinga Abaja near Big Bend, Texas, they left behind a desolate cemetery as well. If anyone knew the story of these anonymous graves and their simple markers, the tale has been forgotten. It's been 50 years since most of those who lived here moved on.*

❈ ❈

Right: *The task of coaxing water from a groaning pump and fetching bucketsful inside often fell on a pioneer family's older children. Much to the youngsters' dismay, water had to be carried for washing, cooking, and drinking. Even the most rambunctious worked at walking carefully without spilling a drop. The water carriers were thankful that mother insisted on regular baths only during the warmer months.*

Ropes, iron brands, and rough-hewn corrals such as this one made up the cowboy's tools on the Arizona range. Cattle ranches still claim huge holdings in the West, but the days of the roundup are long past. The San Francisco Mountains—with the Grand Canyon State's highest peak at over 12,000 feet—rise in the distance.

❋ ❋

All, all, are sleeping on the hill.

—Edgar Lee Masters
"Spoon River Anthology"

Opposite page: *Alexander and Clara MacGregor homesteaded this mountain ranch in Colorado more than a century ago. Their daughter donated the spread to be used as a living history museum so that youngsters could have a firsthand look at the rigors of ranch life in those early days. The ranch, snowbound much of the year at an elevation of 7,500 feet, raises Black Angus cattle, while elk roam in the pastures.*

Above: *Abandoned mine buildings jostle on the slopes near the onetime boom town of Cripple Creek, Colorado. Experts labeled this area worthless, but amateur prospectors using pitchforks and whatever else was handy discovered gold. This town boomed to a population of 25,000, and 500 mines operated at the height of the rush. Nearby Victor, another mining town, literally boasted streets lined with gold; low-grade ore was so plentiful that it was used for paving.*

Above: *A giant load of hay moves more easily by horse-drawn sleigh near Jackson Hole, Wyoming. In this snow-bound region, sleighs travel where motorized vehicles can't. Thanks to a little patience and balancing skill, a load that normally might require two trips glides across the frozen landscape. More than 16 feet of white stuff can pile up during a winter in this mountain country.*

Opposite page: *Frosty white blankets a mountain farm near Granby, Colorado, and piles up along the edges of a country road. Snow may slow things down in this high territory, but plows keep the byways passable. A fresh dusting almost daily obligingly ensures that snow cover glistens as pure as the clouds that float overhead.*

Weather-beaten facades in Leadville, a Colorado mining town, have seen their share of outlandish successes and desperate failures. The "Unsinkable Molly Brown" made her fortune here. Residents have come to cherish the town's checkered past, preserving the character of buildings like this one in the historic district.